Downsizing
with
Family History
in Mind

Other Books by Devon Noel Lee

21st Century Family Historian

Power Scrapbooking

Family History Scrapbooking Simplified

From Metal to Rhinestones: A Quest for the Crown

Other Books by Andrew Lee

How to Fail English with Style

Other Books by Devon Noel Lee & Andrew Lee

DNA Q&A

Reimagine Family History

A Recipe for Writing Family History

Downsizing

with

Family History

in Mind

**Devon Noel Lee
& Andrew Lee**

Downsizing with Family History in Mind

Published by FHF Group LLC

Table of Contents

This book is dedicated to all who find treasures in mountains of stuff.

Introduction

Families face downsizing at mansnuglyrent times in their lives including death, health, moves, family re-combinations, financial changes, anusableepare against disaster. More often than not, few people focus on counter top.rm goal of preserving family treasures when reducing their household items. If they do, they preserve too little, too much, or not the right things.

In December 2012, I faced a downsizing emergency. My mother had died in Texas while I lived in Iowa. Over the course of a week, I had to fly from Iowa to the Lone Star State, arrange the funeral, attend the funeral, and preserve the most valuable of my mother's possessions. When I boarded the plane to return home, whatever remained behind became charitable donations.

My mother had so many possessions, even after downsizing from a 3-bedroom home to an apartment a few years before. Over the course of our lives, we all collect stuff that has meaning to us. My Mom was no exception. I struggled deciding what to keep and what to leave behind.

Decades before, my mother had started keeping family records. I had sweet talked my mother into giving me the genealogical records a few years earlier. My home and computer back in Iowa housed many key family documents and photos.

Despite having already received the majority of the genealogical treasures, I still faced a mountain of stuff. Mother had a three-foot-tall stack of photo albums that had not been digitized. The apartment contained additional memorabilia that could never fit in my two suitcases. Shipping these items back to Iowa would have cost a small fortune. In the end, I made decisions, hard decisions, in a very short amount of time. I still wonder about and reflect on whether I made the correct decisions.

Why Do We Downsize?

For many people, the decision to downsize their home is thrust upon them. Perhaps they become ill and need to move into a long-term care facility. Sometimes, a change in employment or living on a fixed income triggers a downsize. Many individuals and families live beyond their means and the debt monster finally catches up to them, forcing the need to reduce their possessions. Most of these health and financial upheavals carry an emotional burden along with the need to simplify their lives.

Sometimes people have to downsize after the death of a loved one. They must rush into a house and quickly save what they can for posterity's sake. They will sell everything else and put the house on the market to settle the estate. If the loved one resided in an apartment or rental unit, the timeline to clear out the possessions significantly decreases.

Sometimes people consciously choose to downsize. Perhaps they want to live in a more desirable neighborhood, but the high price tag means less square footage. Maybe they want to live in an urban environment that is light on household living space but big on external amenities. Some individuals want to live in a retirement community with maid service! Others downsize so they can travel the world and do not need to have a 3,000 square-foot house full of trinkets and furniture they will not view for months on end.

On a smaller scale, some individuals inherit a mountain of genealogical information from a relative. They wish to decrease the pile before an avalanche takes over. Sometimes that information is organized and others it is more of a jumbled mess that looks as if it was thrown together.

Downsizing happens to people of all ages and for a vast number of reasons. In downsizing, families or individuals must decrease the volume of the possessions that they have accumulated for 10, 20, 50 or more years! Space dictates the amount of reduction that must happen. The new living space lacks enough space to keep everything.

A Small Apartment Forced Our First Downsize

After we married, Andy and I had to move all of my possessions from my parent's home in Houston to our 550 square foot apartment in College Station. Andy brought few things into the marriage, so I thought I would have enough space for my keepsakes. Reality soon kicked me in the gut.

I had a mind for preserving my personal history since a very early age. I had boxes and boxes in my parent's garage, even though that is one of the worst places to store valuables. My knowledge of proper preservation would come later.

Andy regarded the volume of boxes with dumbfounded astonishment. He quickly realized my possessions would not fit in our tiny apartment, if we wanted space to eat and sleep. I had to downsize. We only had the weekend to do it.

We pulled all boxes, and boxes, and boxes onto the front walkway early Saturday morning. We quickly filled up the walkway, spilled over onto the yard, and then the driveway. As we started sifting through what to keep and what to toss, people started stopping by. Can you guess what they asked?

"Are you having a yard sale?"

I could not believe the nerve of those people. Why were they stopping? Did it look like a garage sale? I had no tables displaying my wares. Go away!

When the anger subsided, shock set in. I realized that I had nothing of value to sell. I had a mountain of junk. I could then move forward with downsizing because I only wanted to keep valuable items.

We reduced my 30 boxes with keepsakes from my first 20 years to a half dozen boxes. We drove an entire truckload of stuff to the dump.

After downsizing to those few boxes, do I remember what went to the dump? Better yet, do I miss anything in those boxes?

I only regret not saving a few items. I wish I had taken pictures of my magazines. I would love to have saved my sticker collection to add to scrapbooks of my childhood or let my girls use them in their craft projects. Other than that, I feel no guilt for taking the clutter to the dumpster.

Devon's Mom's First Downsize

After my Dad died, Mother downsized from a 3 bedroom home to a one-room studio apartment. Mom wanted to know if I wanted to have anything from her house before she reduced her possessions. Having already experienced a downsizing process, I replied with a hasty no.

Since the weekend sorting my things, Andy and I have lived a more minimalist lifestyle. I did not want my mother's furniture, salt and pepper shakers, stuffed bear collection, China, or business papers. However, I did want the genealogical papers and photos.

Mom mailed a few photo albums and most of the genealogical records. She kept a few boxes of genealogy treasures, including the Geiszler Family Bible.

After ten years, I still would not want any of my mother's furniture, bear collection, or business papers. I might want one salt and pepper shaker set. She did have one or two pieces of the family china I miss. Yet, where would I have put it?

I regret not preserving my mother's hobbies, business, and my heritage through photography and scanning. I kick myself for not recording why she collected her bears and the story behind each one. I regret not forcing mom to give me the Geiszler Family Bible. When she moved to her small apartment, she improperly stored the bible and it deteriorate beyond repair.

I have regretted my hasty answer when mom asked if I wanted anything from her home. I wish I had saved the memories even though I didn't want the things. I would have preserved more of my family legacy.

What should happen?

Downsizing your possessions should fall somewhere in the middle between tossing out things you will never miss and trashing those things you will kick yourself for not saving. This is the cross section where we preserve our family history while clearing out the clutter.

You have to plan ahead. It's often said that:

"Failing to plan is planning to fail."

You need a plan. A single plan is not going to work for everyone. This book will share guiding principles that will enable you to develop your own plan. Before we discuss those principles, we need to define the objectives for downsizing with family history in mind.

KEEP THIS IN MIND
Not everyone's plan will be the same, but the end result will be preserved family history and your treasures.

Who Needs to Downsize?

What a loaded question.

Most people need to reduce the amount of stuff they have collected. The better question should be, "When do most people downsize?"

Receiving a Genealogical Inheritance (or Clutter in 1,000 boxes)

For some, inheriting boxes of genealogy would not trigger the need to downsize. However, when the family archive migrates from one person to the next, the collection grows to an overwhelming mass that quashes any excitement.

Inherited genealogy collections often include documents, photographs, diaries, books, and research notes. Other family legacy collections include trinkets, heirlooms, clothing, and assorted keepsakes. While sentimental items and random notes with limited value pepper nearly every family archive.

The amount of physical space that the family archive consumes varies greatly. Some archives fill entire rooms with file cabinets full of binders, books, piles, and photo albums. Other collections can fit into a suitcase that can fit in the overhead bin of an airplane, but probably should not because of it's weight. As an heir receives their inheritance, their homes, garages, attics, and basements fill up with other people's stuff.

"Who has room for all of this stuff?" a disgruntled spouse will say to their genealogy loving partner as they haul in the family history windfall. Truth be told, the disgruntled spouse's complaints contain merit. Unless you have an empty 4,500 square foot home with a climate control room for all of the new genealogical material, you probably need to downsize.

Folks who receive a small box of genealogical material do not receive an exemption from the need to downsize. Often genealogy files and photo albums filling three large crates can rapidly be decreased to one photo album and two file folders after sorting the material.

Reducing Your Living Situation

Whether by compulsion or by choice, many individuals will decrease their living spaces and face the need to reduce their possessions. Often, downsizing your home is less challenging because of your familiarity with the items in your home. For instance, you know you can live without three can openers when one will accomplish the job. You never reduced your possessions because you lacked a pressing need.

The hardest part of the process involves determining the degree of emotional attachment you have to items that invoke memories. Sometimes you know too much about your possessions. You may struggle with guilt that prevents you from giving things new homes which will enable you to fit into your new living situation.

Your goal should be to focus on reducing your possessions to accommodate the square footage in your new living space without sacrificing your memories or your family history. Additionally, you seek to avoid purchasing additional storage.

Reducing the Living Situation of Another

Reducing the contents of an entire house or apartment of someone else has its own challenges. When de-cluttering another person's home, you can often place an accurate measure on the value of their furniture, clothes, jewelry, and miscellaneous household goods. However, evaluating memorabilia and sentimental items slows down the process due to fear of discarding the wrong things.

Additionally, many people face a time crunch when downsizing someone's estate (no matter how small). The emotional trials of losing someone recently or knowing they will soon depart this earth makes clearing out their possessions not for the faint of heart. Nostalgic moments that happen when processing keepsakes will steal the time you need to process their possessions and may cloud your judgment.

When working with others to downsize a family member's home, people have different ideas of value. Add the variations in temperament and emotions, and downsizing seems impossible. Family members may argue over what to keep, save, and give to family members. Feuds break as people shout:

"She took the wedding ring that I wanted!"

"He took daddy's cowboy hat which dad promised to me!"

"Why does he get the military medals when I served in the military and would appreciate them more!"

Hostilities increase, tears flow, and you want to strike a match and burn the place down. Or, to avoid arson charges, you say, "the heck with it."

Why is downsizing so difficult?

When a business downsizes, management cannot take the employee list, cross off every third name, and then expect that the company will run smoothly. Downsizing employees takes a tremendous amount of time to do it well. Each department must have the proper amount of resources for the current and projected workload after the staff reduction. In the end, management needs to make the tough call to lay off some people who may have years of experience and have been a great asset to the company.

Similarly, downsizing a home and the family archive should not employ the unwise approach of tossing out every third box in the attic or dumping every second cabinet in the trash heap. Downsizing with family history in mind requires care and wise judgment so that a family legacy remains. Time and emotions tend to work against us when downsizing.

Time Challenges

When downsizing, most people do not always have the luxury of time. Even when they do, few spend their time wisely. Downsizing takes time, sometimes an inordinate amount of time to do it well. Thousands of items and documents need to be examined, evaluated and processed.

If you have 6-12 months to downsize, you will probably decrease your things in the last 2-3 months. If you wait until the last moment, you will likely downsize with reckless abandon or not at all.

For those with shorter timelines, you have to face the reality that you lack time to do everything you want. You may wish to donate to the best possible location that will love the things you no longer have the space to keep. However, the donation process may take more time that you have allotted. Many things may have to be done in haste, in order to get through the short process.

Emotional Obstacles

If time is enemy number one, emotions come in as a close second, if not a tie. As mentioned earlier, nostalgia clouds your evaluation of value and ability to make judgments. You can not allow your emotions, or those of others, to prevent you from removing things from your care.

Sorting through a household, or file cabinet can trigger memories that you wish to explore and relive. It can trigger tears over the loved ones who have recently passed. Anger may rear its ugly head over the fact that you have to downsize at all!

Be aware of the roller coaster of emotions. Take breaks if you need them, but then press on with the hope of keeping the things that matter most.

Three ways people typically downsize

Although time and emotions constrain the ability of individuals to downsize, many methods of reducing excess stuff create problems for preserving family history.

"Box, What Box?" - Method

People often put off downsizing a home or a collection until it is too late to make wise decisions. So they do not make decisions.

If the item is out of sight, you forget it exists. Surely a storage unit or shed could be used to hide the family archive. When forced to downsize, often the avoidance method tosses everything in the garbage without a second glance.

In time, the out of sight out of mind items will lose their value and make their way to a landfill or bonfire unless a genealogically minded individual comes to the rescue. But those family history heroes have to know an archive needs rescuing before they can step up to the challenge.

"I Can't Let it Go" - Method

Many people clearing out their home or that of a loved one will purchase storage units or give up their garage to house all of the items from that other home. They will toss out expired food and beauty products, maybe.

Instead of evaluating their possessions, they will find a way for everything to fit in their smaller living situation. Chances are the living room and guest bedroom will soon become too cluttered to enjoy. Additionally, avoid walking into the garage unless you want to find yourself lost for a week.

"Throw It All Out!" - Method

It seems some folks hear the word downsize and they start carting everything out for trash pick up day or to the nearest dumpster. They act rashly thinking nothing has value.

Some folks are not that rash. Instead, they attempt to sell every portrait, knife, and bookcase in hopes of making a quick buck, pay off debts in the estate, or use it for their future lifestyle.

If anything does not sell, they will pack up any available vehicle and drive over to a donation center to clear the clutter.

In short, the hasty individual does not preserve their family history well, if at all. A few years later, they may wish they had used more caution in disposing of the family treasures. If they fall in love with genealogy, they will pine for the family bible that they tossed into the trash heap.

What is your method?

Considering these three common methods, which one describes you best? Hopefully, you will say, none of those! Instead, you like, or will learn to appreciate, planning ahead. To become a planner, you may need to change the way you think.

> ## GET YOUR HEAD
> ## IN THE GAME

This phrase has been popular since a Disney movie had the main character remind himself to stay focused while playing basketball. You need to stay focused while downsizing with family history in mind. To do that, let's go through the six mind shifts you will need to adopt to keep your head in the game of reducing wisely.

Mind Shift #1: Get Over the Guilt

Before you read another page, you have to learn one simple fact.

When you do it well, you feel no guilt in downsizing

You really can give away the cute crafts your child made 20 years ago. You really can give away the china, the armoire, the wing-back chairs, and the handwritten genealogical charts. If needed, you will find a way to preserve the data and the memories first, but you really can let go. Do not feel guilty when you make a value judgment about parting with things in your home or family archive.

Mind Shift #2: Today is Someday

If you have fallen into the trap of keeping things that will be useful someday, today is that future day. Use it up, wear it out, or throw it away.

Donate the craft items that you have not used to a classroom or group that will appreciate them. The clothing, serving dishes, appliances, and other items around your home that you have not used in years should leave your home today.

I had done a lot of painting and other crafty things with my children when they were younger. As they have grown older, the paints, and stamps, and other knickknacks piled up and collected dust. One day, I posted a message on our community Facebook page offering the craft items. In a couple of hours, I had an elementary school teacher on my doorstep taking two boxes of craft supplies off my hands. While she was happy for the free supplies, I celebrated having fewer dust collectors in my home.

Stop saving china and dinnerware for special occasions. Today is that special occasion. Use these dishes as your daily dishes because few heirs want your china sets.

Growing up, Andy's mother had a china set, which included crystal glasses and sterling silverware, that she only used once a month for a Sunday meal. His parents received this set on their wedding day, and they treasured it to the point of rarely using the gift. Andy and his brothers viewed the china and silverware as a hassle. It represented extra chores of hand washing taking special care to make sure nothing broke. When his parents asked if any of the boys wanted the china, they all declined. Suddenly their treasured china set became worthless. Additionally, they could not find buyers on Craig's List or eBay for the set either.

Downsizing focuses on eliminating anything that is not useful today. Downsizing with family history in mind discards anything that clutters up your family legacy.

Mind Shift #3: Grab the Tissues

Downsizing generates emotional overload. When my in-laws downsized their home to start traveling the world, they indicated the intensity of memories flooding their senses. They could not make decisions about their household goods in the few short months before their moving day. They did a great first pass, but still, they had truckloads of items stuffed in our attic.

After a year overseas, they returned to their things and began an aggressive downsizing campaign. Time away from the emotional intensity gave them the perspective they needed to downsize. They were much more successful in their reduction attempts.

You may not have time to step away from your things to gain perspective. Take a breather, use a tissue, and then continue.

Mind Shift #4: Planning Ahead Reduces the Overwhelm

Many people consider downsizing an overwhelming task. Reviewing every paper, every household good, every artifact, or every photo consumes time and drains energy. The shorter your timeline and larger your household's collection, the more draining and overwhelming the task becomes.

Think of it like a math problem.

$$O = \frac{S}{T * P}$$

O equals the level of overwhelm you feel. **S** equals the amount of stuff you have to downsize. **T** equals the time you have to downsize. **P** equals the amount of planning you have done.

If **S** goes up and **T** goes down, you end up with a very large **O**.

It does not have to be so.

We will cover some planning principles (the **P** in the equation) that you can put into place to help you make better decisions in the time you have allotted. The task is still sizable, but manageable. Having a thought out plan (**P**) can decrease the overwhelm (**O**) even when stuff (**S**) is large and time (**T**) is small.

Mind Shift #5: Your Possessions Do Not Provide Comfort

Hoarders often return to their pack rat ways because surrounding themselves with so much stuff creates a sense of security. The comfort from possessions might stem from an impoverished childhood. A house full of things may depict wealth, especially for those who lived during the Great Depression.

The volume of stuff in your home will never provide you the comfort you need. The quality of your possessions will. When you downsize with family history in mind, you will reduce down to the treasures with the most sentimental value and showcase them. Why block the view with low-value items?

Mind Shift #6: End the Decision Paralysis

Ultimately, downsizing is hard when you can not make a decision. You lack the knowledge for evaluating an item from a long-term perspective. This book will help you overcome the paralysis by pointing out the categories of stuff you should keep, process, giveaway, and discard entirely.

When you can not make a decision, you will have a handy reference guide to help you move past the sticking points.

How does a genealogist downsize?

There are memes on the internet that say genealogists provide validation to hoarding. Many involved in family history work are borderline neurotic in their pack rat ways; however, a wise genealogist always streamlines and downsizes what they collect with an eye toward preservation.

The family archives that will stand the test of time, will preserve the most sentimental valuables in quality boxes but keep the collection small. The family archivist will also convert their data and documents into books, showpieces, and digital media with stories for all to enjoy.

Additionally, genealogists who continually downsize discover how the process improves their research. They will spend less time repeating tasks that they have already completed. They will have their research in an easily accessible and transferable format. As such, their ability to analyze their research, any time and anywhere, increases. They may also notice significant improvements in the discoveries they find.

Do you really need to keep all this stuff?

Do not continue to leave valuable items stuck in your closets, attics, garages, and storage units. The items lose their value (and sometimes deteriorate) when you do.

When downsizing focuses on reduction while preserving family history, you will save what matters most, find better homes for other valuables, and dispose of the items that are of little importance now and in the future.

Why De-cluttering Does Not Work

With your head in the game and your tissue box close at hand, you are ready to begin downsizing with family history in mind. Before you create your plan, recognize why most de-cluttering methods fail.

Common De-cluttering Practices are Horrible

Numerous articles, books, and televisions shows recommend downsizing by sorting your possessions into KEEP, SELL, and DONATE piles. The experts fail to teach you how to evaluate your wares and keepsakes beyond their functionality for the present. Not everything in your home serves a utilitarian purpose right now. Without proper instruction on evaluating sentimental items, many people place all keepsakes in the KEEP pile.

The three-box method also lacks a box for items that you need to process before discarding. This box would only contain things you will keep long enough to preserve in a digital file. After digitization, drop the item into a donate pile.

Finally, the three-box method rarely has a trash pile. Few people realize that many possessions belong in the trash, beyond last night's take out containers. Embrace the trash can to downsize successfully. Broken, moldy, or valueless items need a one-way ticket to the landfill.

Don't Do It On The Lawn

Every hoarding, downsizing or de-cluttering TV show force the disorganized participants to sort their possessions into those three piles on the front lawn or in their garage. A crew will pull everything out of a home and arrange it in the yard or garage. Opposite the household mountain sits three piles with "Keep," "Sell," and "Donate" emblazoned on attractive signs.

As the participants sift through their mountain of possessions, the sell and donate, piles remain minuscule. Hopefully, they throw a few things in the trash. The keep pile appears untouched.

After the first sorting, an expert shakes their head with shame as they criticize the participants for not reducing their possessions enough. Does this attitude help anyone de-clutter or downsize? NO! They need guidelines and assistance.

Guidelines Help Evaluate the Value of Possessions

In this book, you will evaluate items, such as heirloom furniture, clothing, household goods, documents, photos, and other keepsakes, from the family history preservation perspective. We will leave the determination of what to keep based on functionality to the typical downsizing guru.

This book will teach you how to review your household items not only in terms of what can be physically saved but what to preserve digitally. Utilizing technology to digitally preserve your family history further enables you to reduce your space requirements for physical storage.

In the end, you will know how to evaluate anything that has sentimental or historical value. You'll recognize the different degrees of sentimentality and that not every degree deserves space in your home.

Downsizing Advice You Can Ignore

"Contain yourself to just one memorabilia box that's easy to store out of sight."

Not every memorabilia item worth keeping fits into one box. Valuable items stored out of site lose their value over time. You should preserve the things that have high sentimental value, that you are willing to display.

"90% of what is in the loft is trash."

You store many items in the loft, or storage unit, because you will dig them out when you want or need them. Upon closer inspection, you may discover that many items in the loft have more value than the items that reside in your current living space. Do not use an off-hand comment to decide what to keep or throw out.

"Discard anything that you didn't remember was there."

How often have you dug through your storage and said, "I forgot I had this!"? Things such as jewelry that belonged to a mother, grandmother, or aunt fall into this category. Photographs and genealogically significant documents do as well. Should you throw those out because you had forgotten their existence? No.

"Discard large items that take up too much room and could be borrowed if you ever need them again."

This advice confuses size with functionality. Keep large items that you have the means to keep and has significant historical value. Additionally, do not allow small things, that you can borrow if you ever need them again, to clutter your home.

"Throw anything that makes you feel sad or guilty when you look at it."

Emotions should not determine whether you keep or discard something. Care Bears make me happy, but should I keep them? I had a love/hate relationship with my mother's newsletter business. Should I dispose of all of her printed issues? What if you have something from a parent who passed away and you feel guilty for how you last spoke to one another before they died, should you throw out anything that reminds you of that? Instead, base decisions on the functional or family history value an item has.

"Discard any earrings that don't have their partner."

Sentimentality might overrule functionality in terms of family history and negate this de-cluttering tip. Jewelry and earrings that have limited functionality (such as having a missing match, a broken clasp, and missing watch band), may still offer a key to unlock the past. Additionally, some of these small pieces can be placed in a shadow box or reset as a necklace or a ring.

"Throw out mugs or glasses over the total number of people you would ever have drinking in your home in one go."

This statement goes to functionality rather than someone's desire to have a collection. Depending upon the collection (mugs, glasses, china, salt & pepper shakers, shot glasses, wine goblets, beer steins), perhaps your collection should be reduced to 3, 6, 9, or 10 for aesthetic pleasantry. If you live alone, your collection ignores the 'expert' de-cluttering advice.

"Throw out CDs & DVDs you haven't watched and won't listen to again."

Technology has changed, and many of us no longer have the ability to play CDs or DVDs. Follow this advice only after you first make a note of what you did enjoy and why. Then discard the CDs and DVDs, along with VHS cassettes and cassette recordings of non-family history value.

"Discard change jars."

I dislike the advice to throw out change jars completely. My grandfather had numerous giant wine jugs that he stuffed with pennies, dimes, and nickels. Many people would say, cash in the contents and recycle the glass. But if I could have anything, other than the photos that hung on my grandparent's home, I wish I could have one of those glass jugs full of money to remember him by.

The jars also have historical significance. During the Great Depression and the war years, many people started stashing coins in these jars. The jars became the saver's 'emergency fund' or their donation to the war efforts. The jars represented security and the history of that time. Be cautious. One coin jar might be worth saving as a physical item, the remainder of the collection is worth photographing.

As you can see, the de-cluttering advice available contains numerous statements that fail upon closer inspection. This book helps you focus on downsizing while preserving your family legacy.

A Better Way to Downsize

Instead of following the typical paths of downsizing, which rarely focus on preserving your family legacy, this chapter focuses on a better method of possession reduction. There are four principles to downsizing with family history in mind: reduce, preserve, reclaim, and showcase.

Chapters throughout this book will feature each principle. Since the principle of "Reduce" deals with decision making, it appears in the most chapters. For now, let us review the steps at a high-level.

Reduce

Downsizing means making something smaller. In this case, reducing your household's accumulation of furnishing, clothing, keepsakes, documents, and more.

If you are reducing a household, you will decrease the amount of furnishings and household items. You will reduce the hundreds of boxes of keepsakes down to a minimal collection to keep your heart happy while clearing out the clutter. You will also clean out your attics, closets, garages, and all other hidden storage near your home as well. Ultimately, you will eliminate any off-site storage.

If you inherited someone else's possessions or genealogy collection, you are going to reduce what you keep to the fewest boxes possible and incorporate anything else into your treasures.

If you can not decide whether to keep or cull something from your possessions, save the item until you have completed the next step. At some point, your decision will become apparent and guilt free.

Preserve

After you have initially culled the collection, you are going to preserve the memories and stories of your family. You will preserve treasures physically and others digitally.

When you have digitally preserved your family history, you can organize the physical items that will remain in your home. You must label what you keep to retain their value.

After you captured your belongings in digital form, you will often discover you no longer need to store it in your home. Set these items aside for the steps in the 'reclaim' principle.

Reclaim

With your possessions preserved, organized and stored, you can finish reclaiming the space in your home. You will give things away, attempt to sell anything of value, or discard the rest.

The spaces in your home will not overflow with valueless items. You will reclaim every area in your home for things that have function and family legacy. You will likely reduce five bookcases for your souvenirs in your living room to one curio cabinet. The guilt decreases as your space increases because you have preserved with family history in mind.

Showcase

As you enjoy your new space or incorporate your inheritance into your home, surround yourself with value-rich items or free yourself to have nothing! Showcase the things that bring you the most joy and connect you to your loved ones. When someone needs to process your household after you die, they will have more success because you've only kept things that have the richest value for the future.

The Four Principles are Intertwined

Recognize that the reduce, preserve, reclaim and showcase are not independent, sequential steps. They are intertwined principles that support each other and may happen simultaneously.

As you reduce what you have, you'll reclaim spaces in your home. After you preserve your treasures, you'll showcase what you love most. If you can't showcase an item, you'll give it away and reclaim your space. As you showcase items, you may discover you can reduce your collections even further. Remember that the principles work together rather than separately.

With this high-level overview complete, let us focus on learning how to make decisions, pick an action plan based on your needs, and downsize with family history in mind.

REDUCE: Principles of Evaluating Your Possessions

KEEP, SELL and DONATE are meaningless without the ability to evaluate your possessions in terms of their function and family history value. You need guidelines to help simplify the process and increase the chances you will make the correct decisions more often than not. Before we dive into some concrete examples, think about things that are considered of great worth and retain their value over time.

The first thing that comes to my mind is gold. Since the times of Ancient Egypt, pharaohs, priests, and peasants have valued gold. It was rare and shiny, yet easy to work with and form into various shapes by a variety of means. Humans prized gold for both ornamentation and as a store of value. After thousands of years, we still use gold for these purposes.

When we think of having something made of gold or using it in transactions, we may think of the following words:

> Valuable – Precious – Lasting – Investment –
> Prosperity – Commemorative – Useful – Does
> not tarnish

Gold is recognized as a material that is useful for many applications, including but not limited to financial transactions. Gold items are also often used in many ceremonies and honors. Additionally, gold has tremendous value in the past, for the present, and into the future.

Do you know what chrome plastic is?

Few people can readily identify chrome plastic but have seen it and tossed it out more often than they realize. Chrome plastic is a generic plastic item covered with a shiny chrome finish. Think about a toy car and with any reflective shiny parts. The shiny parts are likely chrome plastic. It is useful, but it lacks lasting value like gold.

Can you imagine giving a child a toy car with gold accent pieces?

Nope. The child will damage or lose that toy in a heartbeat, and you would probably freak out. But if they broke or lost a toy with chrome plastic, you will rarely shed tears. The child may, but you will not.

Words that describe chrome plastic include:

Useful – Common – Cheap – Disposable –
Temporary – Breakable

Notice that both gold and chrome plastic have purposes, but one is decidedly more valuable in the long term than the other. Given a choice, would you like a home filled with high-value items, like gold, or limited value items, like chrome plastic?

Every Item is Either Gold or Chrome Plastic

This analogy demonstrates a mental measuring device which you can use when evaluating everything that you own. The analogy helps you decide whether to keep or remove items from your home or collections.

For every downsizing decision you make, you will ask:

Is this item as valuable as gold or chrome plastic?

Will the item retain its value for the long-term or is it useful but disposable?

When you are downsizing with family history in mind, what should you keep?

Keep the gold.

Toss the Chrome Plastic.

Who decides the valuation of each item?

You are the appraiser of the worth of an item. After all, this is your stuff. You know far more about it than we do. There are lots of things that can make something valuable and each person will have different standards that they apply.

The following will either seem logical or bother you to no end. It is okay to disagree with the recommendations in this book and keep something that we identify as chrome plastic. Realize that the people who will inherit your stuff should also think the same as you or they will not cherish it. We hope to shock you into realizing that your family generally regards your possessions as less valuable than you do. Therefore our recommendations may seem harsh.

Also recognize, when you downsize your home, or those of your loved ones, with a focus on saving what many people will find valuable rather than a handful of individuals, you increase the chances that more heirlooms and genealogically important items survive into the future. If you are bogged down with things that 'could have value,' you increase the chances that everything is tossed out – both gold and plastic – in future generations.

Family History Gold

The gold vs. chrome plastic analogy is a great theory, but how can it be applied? Here are three criteria that help you determine if an item is family history gold.

Family history gold is original, unique, and/or, has high sentimental value.

Original items include an original birth certificate rather than a copy made in blue ink from the 1970s. Unique items might be wooden clogs that belonged to a Dutch ancestor who immigrated to Illinois. Items that have high sentimental value would cause heart-wrenching sobs for months if they were ever lost or damaged. It may be a doll you received from your grandmother as a child or a bomber jacket that belonged to your grandfather.

Family History gold should meet one or more of these criteria, preferably more. Here are a few examples to better explain golden treasures:

29

A Family Bible usually fits the requirements of original, unique, and highly sentimental. The Bible should record family events such as births and marriages or have notations of favorite passages or quotes by the owner. Otherwise, it is just a book.

A journal is unique and original if it belonged to a direct ancestor or a close relation, such as an aunt or great uncle. If so, you have family history gold. If the diary pertains to a distant family line, the item is chrome plastic for you but gold to someone with a more direct connection. If you do not know the originator of the journal, it may be gold to someone whose job it is to curate such historical items. Otherwise, it is chrome plastic.

A ten-year-old basket containing plastic grass that our daughter used for her first Easter egg hunt is original, but it is not unique and does not have high sentimental value. It fails the gold vs. chrome plastic test.

A crown or tiara could be gold if you know the story behind it.

I won the title *Miss San Jacinto Teen USA* and received a tiara. The tiara is not unique because many young women around the United States wore that crown style. A replacement crown could be purchased online for about $30. However, I would cry buckets if I lost the tiara I received when I won the title. Therefore it is highly sentimental and a piece of gold in our family history.

Some crowns have no story and were used in dress up play. These shiny headpieces do not pass the gold standard test.

Family History Chrome Plastic

In contrast to the gold standard of original, unique and highly sentimental, *chrome plastic items are copies (especially paper copies), easily replaced (primarily through online sources), and/or have limited sentimental value.*

Since the 1950s, our homes have been filled with a lot of disposable items. Clothes are not meant to last long. Furniture is not built to endure. Most members of the MTV generation and Millenials, cringe when thinking about fine china and prefer cheaper dinnerware if they eat at home at all.

Many of our keepsakes also have marginal sentimental value. We kept items because someday it might be valuable. Thousands of children in the 80s started collecting baseball cards, knowing that their collection would one day be worth millions (because their father's collection which was thrown out by their grandmother would have been worth that much). The collections never attained those lofty values, because everyone was keeping them. There was no uniqueness or scarcity in the baseball card market.

Don't Let Chrome Plastic Gifts Become Burdens

Within your household items, you will encounter gifts from your wedding, the birth of children, and so on. Many people hold on to gifts because they imagine the giver will expect to see these displayed when they visit. Do not let gifts have this power over what you keep and what you give away.

Unless a gift giver pays you to store and maintain their gift, they have no say in what you have in your home. A gift is yours to do with as you please. Keep only things in your home and family archive that you will treasure and use.

Chrome Plastic Disguised as Gold

Chrome plastic can often masquerade as gold. The value of an item becomes apparent once it is digitally preserved. If anything quickly loses its value once you have photographed or scanned it, then the item is chrome plastic. Gold still holds its value even after it has been digitized. When you have a questionable item, it is okay to set it in a "To Process" pile and reserve your final evaluation until you have preserved the item. We will talk more about digitization in the chapter *PRESERVE: Digitize Your Family History.*

Occasionally, you will have items that are family history gold, but not to you. If anything becomes valuable when given to someone else, then it is chrome plastic, and you need to find a new home for the item quickly. We discuss this in more detail in the chapter *RECLAIM: Gain Space By Giving Away.*

Many people who attend our classes have also mentioned items that could be gold if something is done to the item to give it more value. For instance, photos that are not labeled and grandma's broken china from Sweden top the list. If you are willing and able to spend the time to mark the unlabeled photos and repair the fractured china, set these items in a "To Process" pile.

Realize that when you are downsizing, time may be critical. You might not have the time or resources to deal with the transformative tasks. Be realistic. Do you really have the time and resources to fix broken items or find missing family details?

Finally, chrome plastic disguised as gold may include items which two people disagree about the value. If you think something is chrome plastic and another person thinks it is gold, give it to the person who values the item. If you believe the item is gold and another person thinks it is chrome plastic, be sure you understand why the other person thinks it has no value. Perhaps you are wrong.

If you still think you are right and have the space and room for the disputed item, then keep it. Recognize others might not find the value in this item if you do not find a way to enhance its value, which we will discuss this in the chapter *SHOWCASE: Display What You Love*.

Four Downsizing Sorting Piles

With the concept of gold and chrome plastic in your mind, use the following actionable guidelines to sift through your belongings, or those from a loved one. In the next few chapters, we share guidelines focused on household items and then genealogically relevant pieces.

As you sift through your possessions, sort your gold and chrome plastic items into one of the following four categories:

Keep – These are the family history gold. You will move these with you to your new space or absorb them into your current home.

Process – Some chrome plastic items need to be processed. You will discard these items after you transfer information to a new medium.

Give Away – Some chrome plastic is gold in another relatives' home or in an archive or repository. These items will leave your house but hopefully be a treasured addition elsewhere.

Trash – Some chrome plastic has lost its value and can quickly be trashed. Embrace the trash can (or the recycling bin if you prefer).

As you sort through your household and inherited genealogy with family history in mind, you will have more success in making wise downsizing decisions. You will find joy in the number of boxes, drawers, and filing cabinets you empty.

REDUCE: Evaluate Your Household Items

With a clear focus of preserving your family legacy, you can downsize your belongings. For the most part, your home contains four categories of possessions:

1. Furniture, Housewares, and Home Decor
2. Clothing and Personal Effects
3. Lifestyle Items
4. Items of Genealogical and Sentimental Value

This chapter will focus on the first three categories. Subsequent chapters will discuss what other downsizing books lack, guidelines for downsizing items of genealogical and sentimental value. We will also share some added insights for preserving items from the first three categories that may benefit your family history.

As stated in the previous chapter *Principles for Evaluating and Reducing Your Possessions*, you will sort your belongings into four piles:

Keep - These are your family history gold.

Process - Mostly chrome plastic disguised as gold.

Give Away - Gold to someone else.

Trash - Chrome plastic

Furniture, Housewares, and Home Decor

For the most part, furniture, housewares, and home decor fall into the chrome plastic category. Many large furnishings such as chairs, sofas, recliners, beds, and nightstands have served their purposes. You can now sell them in an estate sale, garage sale, or donate them to charity. Only keep what will fit in your smaller living space.

When you examine antique and family heirlooms, do not feel obligated to keep any item. One friend of ours refused to part with a wooden chest of drawers because it belonged to an ancestor. When asked about the identity of the original owner and the history behind the chest, she could not name the ancestor. This item resembles a purchase from an antique shop if you can not identify the original owner and your relationship to them. As such, you should discard any furnishing in which family members have forgotten the story behind the item.

The fastest way to determine the historical value of furniture and household items is to ask these three questions:

1. Do I know the story behind the piece?
2. Do I know who originally owned the piece?
3. Do I know who owned it between the original owner and myself?

If you can not answer these questions with a strong family story, then you have chrome plastic, and it is time to let someone else enjoy the furnishings, housewares, or home decor items.

What should you do with broken or damaged furnishings?

Carefully consider broken china or other household items which may require repair work. If the fractured piece is valuable without repair, such as a cuckoo clock, then evaluate it as you would other household furnishings.

If the item needs repairs and you are willing to spend the time and energy or money to restore it, then set it aside until the sorting process is complete. Just make sure the repair pile is small.

Discard any item you do not wish to repair or hire someone to refurbish. You may need to review your repair pile and re-ask yourself whether the things are really worth fixing.

Action Steps:

Before you downsize, photograph the living space and the furnishings. Then proceed to decrease the belongings. Do not keep more than you have space. If the number of belongings you wish to save requires additional storage facilities to maintain, keep reducing.

Keep: Only keep the furnishings which have significant family history value and fit in your new living space. Opt for functionality over sentimentality

Process: If an item is broken or damaged and you will repair it soon, set it aside and have it fixed quickly.

Give Away: If you are downsizing a loved one's home, sell or donate the vast majority of the furnishings.

Trash: Discard anything broken or damaged, and you do not wish to repair.

What about...?

While presenting this book as a workshop, many participants still have questions regarding the family history value of items in their family archive. We offer these suggestions for the specific items others have asked us about:

An Antique Spinning Wheel – Unless your family business currently includes seamstresses and tailors, the spinning wheel is likely chrome plastic. It could be gold to a collector or a museum if you have the time to find such an interested recipient.

Antique Furniture – Apply the three questions listed above to decide if the antiques should stay in the family. Otherwise, find new owners for the furniture either in your home or in a stranger's home. You could also ask an antique shop if they would accept the piece. You may also discover some furnishings most often find their way to the trash pile.

Furniture From Your Relatives – Regardless of whether the furniture comes from your grandparents, your in-laws, or your mother-in-law's ex-boyfriend, furniture which you no longer use has lost its value. Eliminate those pieces from your home.

Wicker Rocker That Was Grandmother's Wedding Gift – Pieces like these belonged to a specific individual with a known story. Keep it if this piece brings you joy and will fit in your new living space. If not, find a new home for it within your extended family.

Christmas Decorations - Reduce your Christmas decorations to the items that have the most memorable stories. Consider photographing all other decorations and then giving them away.

Grandmother's Bread Bowl, Mother's pitcher and bowl, Great-Grandmother's Dinner Set – If you have space, keep these items and use them.

Old Clock, Antique Silver Teapot, Old Cameras – If you do not know the story behind an heirloom, give it away. If an item has sentimental or family history value, photograph it and then decide if you have the space to keep it. You can not keep everything in physical format. You can save every digitized memory. Reduce to the items that bring you the most joy.

Broken dishes, broken family clock, empty photo frames, unmatched kitchen items from Vienna – Place broken pieces into the trash unless you are willing to repair the items within the next month.

Hopefully, this list of specific items helps you clarify the guidelines. If you have more questions about what furnishings to keep or discard, contact us on Facebook, Instagram or Twitter with a photo of the item and your question.

Clothing

Downsizing our own wardrobe or that of a beloved relative has several categories of decisions to make. The guidelines differ depending on if you are downsizing your wardrobe, a historic wardrobe, or the wardrobe that belonged to grandma or a great uncle.

If you must reduce your clothing and personal effects, downsize with an eye toward functionality. Does your wardrobe provide adequate attire for the lifestyle you live and the activities you plan on doing in the near future? Besides your day to day clothes, you may want to keep clothes for special occasions. If you plan on providing some outdoor service or do home repairs, you may need to keep some grubby clothes.

What about sentimental clothing you are saving for a special occasion?

Sentimental wardrobe items include wedding dresses, christening gowns, first communion attire, and the like. Despite the difficulty, realistically evaluate your situation with brutal honesty. Not every sentimental outfit should stay in your possession.

I saved my wedding dress for years thinking it would pass on to our daughters. Our daughters do not have the same body build as I do and have differences in their style preferences. The wedding dress suddenly became chrome plastic. The veil has retained its golden value. Our girls hope to wear the veil when they wed.

Meanwhile, I have the christening gown that my mother hand crocheted. My mother saved it in hopes a granddaughter would wear it. Our eldest daughter wore the blessing gown on her special day. We have kept the dress for a future granddaughter to wear.

If you have clothing you hope a child will wear someday, evaluate whether this will likely happen and choose accordingly.

Some people save sentimental clothing with no hopes of anyone wearing it in the future. The pieces represent an individual's past. This includes costumes, varsity jackets, prom gowns, and sports uniforms. Souvenir clothing also falls into this category. Most of these pieces have lost their value. Photograph the item and then sift it out of your wardrobe and storage.

Action Step:

Keep: Save the clothing you wear often. Keep clothing and personal effects that you use infrequently, has a specific purpose and you can not easily replace, such as a formal gown or funeral dress.

Keep: Save clothing that has an emotional or traditional value that family members want you to retain.

Process: If you have time, photograph clothing with sentimental value and then place them in the give away pile. If you are short on time, photograph only the most essential items.

Give Away: Discard any item you have not worn in 6 months (unless it is seasonal) or that no longer fits.

Give Away: Donate or sell the remaining items.

What about clothing belonging to a loved one?

The clothing of our relatives can cause a heavy dose of nostalgia. The sweaters, jackets, and shirts smell like our relatives, which may or may not be a good thing. Some items evoke specific memories. Some have family history significance. What are you going to do with them?

You can keep a few items that you can use to remember a loved one. For instance, one workshop attendee kept a sweater that belonged to her mother. In so doing, she feels her mother's hug whenever she needs one. Limit yourself to a few items that serve a specific purpose but will not end up in deep storage.

Most of the clothing owned by another will find new homes.

Action Step:

Give Away (Option 1): Donate historically significant items, such as antebellum gowns, pioneer dresses, or Revolutionary War uniforms, to a museum or historical society for use in educating others about the past.

Give Away (Option 2): Ask your relatives if they want any of the military uniforms, cultural attire, christening gowns, etc.

Give Away (Option 3): Let your children and/or grandchildren play with the clothes. My old dance costumes made great dress-up clothes for our daughters.

Give Away (Option 4): Donate the vast majority of your relative's clothing to a charity center. Bag it up and drop it off.

Keep: Save only the pieces that have a family tradition purpose or for which you know the story behind the piece.

What about damaged clothing?

Some clothing items are growing mold or beginning to smell unpleasant, to say the least. For historically significant and ceremonial objects that you wish to keep, you must consider your ability to remove the mold and smells. If you can't, then the item has become chrome plastic and should be trashed. I know this will break your heart, but someone did not preserve the clothing before it fell into disrepair.

Process: Clean and repair clothing that have smells or damage.

Trash: Discard damaged clothing or anything containing mold.

What about...?

Workshop attendees have asked for further clarification on the following items after we mentioned how to reduce clothing:

High School Football Jersey – Classify sports uniforms as chrome plastic. Tough to hear, we know. Photograph them and then let your children and grandchildren play dress up in it.

Blankets and Quilts – We did not mention blankets, but it does fall into textiles. Depending on the quality, creator's identity, and the condition of the blanket or quilt, you can keep it or give it away. Evaluate each blanket and quilt in the same way you would an article of clothing.

Jewelry and Accessories

Similar to clothing, jewelry, shoes, ties, handkerchiefs, belts, and watches have challenges when determining what to keep and what to cull from a household. Not all bracelet,s broaches, earrings, necklaces, pendants, cuff links, and such trinkets have equal value.

As a teenager, I had a lot of jewelry pieces including a James Avery dolphin ring, a James Avery dangle charm ring of a flag twirler, a gold ring with the letter D, to name a few. These pieces decorated my fingers and wrists daily during high school. Since then, I have replaced those rings with my wedding band and my Texas A&M ring. The high school jewelry retains their sentimental value when photographed and then they can be given away.

Some belts with hefty belt buckles (which include rodeo and livestock show championship buckles or those embellished with Harley Davidson logos) may represent family history gold. A young man on the TV show *Relative Race*, who had never met his father, felt connected to him after touching his father's belts and wallet that an ancestor had preserved.

Some jewelry is ringing in family tradition. An engagement ring that has been passed down for several generations comes to mind. However, a wedding band without a story has lost its value. Do not feel lousy selling or giving it away.

Some accessory collections take up too much space. One man had over 200 ties. After his death, the family did not want to keep the neckwear group intact. Instead, they photographed the collection, gave a few neckties to surviving grandchildren and donated the rest to charity.

Costume jewelry rarely retains its value throughout the generations. Andy's grandmother had an extensive collection of costume jewelry. Rather than keep every piece, his mother created a keepsake box with the stones from various rings and necklaces. The keepsake box now has more value than the entire collection.

Action Step:

Reduce jewelry and accessories to save the pieces with the most family history significance. Photograph and give away the rest.

Process: Photograph jewelry and accessory collections as a whole, if the items have sentimental value. If time permits and the individual pieces in the collection warrant, photograph the items individually.

Keep: The most valuable, unique, and/or highly sentimental pieces.

Give Away: Consider sharing jewelry, watches, and handkerchiefs with relatives. Or donate usable items to charity centers.

Trash: Items that are broken or damaged.

What about...?

Workshop attendees have asked for further clarification on how to reduce the following jewelry and accessory pieces:

Jewelry That Belonged to Grandmother – An entire collection of grandma's jewelry does not have to be kept. Keep only the rings, necklaces, pendants, and such that have the most clearly defined stories. Then divide up grandmother's jewelry among her descendants.

Grandfather's Gold Wedding Band – This piece has a more specific story. Whenever you know who owned the item, and why, then you have something small enough to keep. If the ring belonged to a distant relative, consider finding a more direct descendant to receive the item.

Jewelry Boxes – Regardless of who owned the box, it only has value if it has an accompanying story. The fact that a relative owned an item does not force you to keep it. If a jewelry box was a handmade wedding gift created by your grandfather from the money he made mucking stalls during the Great Depression, then you may want to keep it. Be sure to photograph it and record the story behind the jewelry box. Otherwise, consider giving the jewelry box a new home.

Father's Work Hat – Families have fought over work hats! If the hat is small and highly sentimental, keep it. Otherwise, photograph it and discard it. If the hat has historical significance, you could investigate whether a museum would accept it as a donation.

Lifestyle Items

After you downsize home furnishings and clothing, turn your attention to lifestyle items. These include games, crafts, sports equipment, garage tools, lawn equipment, and the trusty backyard grill.

99% of these lifestyle items do not fall into the family history category. But the great thing about lifestyle items, is most of them are conducive to being sold or given away. Reduce these items based on the space you have available in your new home. If you do not have space for a woodworking shop, the tools will need to find new homes. If you do not have space for a closet full of family games, reduce your collection to 2-3 favorites.

When downsizing a loved one's possessions, keep only what you will use. If they had a functional blender and you need a new one, take it. If they had 100 balls of yarn and you crochet ten blankets every year, put these balls to good use. Otherwise, sell or donate nearly all lifestyle items without hesitation.

Books, Games, Movies, Music

When it comes to downsizing, books, games, movies, and music are generally chrome plastic without exception. Many people can access these entertainment options through physical and digital libraries, streaming services, and neighbors.

For both of us, we liked *Where the Sidewalk Ends*, Monopoly, *The Princess Bride*, and CDs by the band Bon Jovi. We do not need to have all of these items in our home. For my parents, they had Louis L'amour books, 8-track tapes, albums, and Parcheesi. I culled these items after my mother passed away.

For family history purposes, a photograph of someone's books, games, movies, and music choices will suffice. Once the picture has persevered their interests, downsize the collection.

The only books worth saving may include family histories, scrapbooks, diaries, and genealogy reference materials. The only movies and music worth preserving feature your ancestors, such as home movies, interviewers, and performances by relatives. Set aside these media items for processing in the chapter *REDUCE: Evaluate Your Photos and Media*.

Keep what you need to function in your new space for a game night or to entertain yourself. Give away the rest, including signed children's books, books featuring a family member as the cover model, and books won during bingo nights at church. You might first wish to photograph the front cover of the book featuring a family member. Then discard the book.

Some items in this category represent family heritage. If you have a unique chess set or Aggravation board, decide who wants these items and gift it to them now. If your relative wrote books that are currently out of print, find an archive or a family member that would like to receive the collection.

In short, gather the books, games, movies, and music into one pile and give them away if you can. Trash them if you can not.

Action Step:

This category of lifestyle items rarely have items worth saving. Rapidly sift through these items and conserve your decision-making time for other types of possessions.

Process: Photograph the media collection.

Give Away: Consider gifting games or books of significant family history to members of your family.

Give Away: Attempt to sell or donate the majority of the books, games, movies, and music.

Trash: Discard any book, game, movie, or music that you can not sell or donate.

Collections

People collect many things from true treasures to faddish items. Some people collect salt and pepper shakers, egg cups, teaspoons, thimbles, Faberge eggs, Christmas ornaments, and china sets. Others collect movie star plates, Care Bears, Star Wars action figures, and vinyl records. Workshop attendees have mentioned their collections of Barbie dolls, porcelain dolls, model cars, Hummel figurines, and Elvis Presley memorabilia. Do you really need to keep all of this stuff?

Regard a small, well-organized collection that brings daily joy as gold. An extensive collection that provides more dust that happiness is chrome plastic. Within many collections, only a handful of pieces have financial or family history value.

My mother assembled an extensive teddy bear collection. One bear wore a replica of my brother's high school band uniform. This bear started the collection and I can identify the story behind the stuffed animal. I could keep the band uniform bear after photographing the remaining to preserve my mother's collection in digital form.

On the flip side, I collected troll dolls, plastic charm necklaces popular in the 80s, and My Little Ponies as a child. After I photographed my childhood treasures, our daughters played with the dolls and ponies and the plastic jewelry went in the trash to eliminate them as choking hazards.

Do not assume every collection has value. Baseball cards collected in the 1980s and 1990s rarely retain their value. A few cards from the earlier years do have a monetary value.

Some family members collected items that would look better in another collector's home or in a museum. A collection of colonial-era artifacts and vintage paintings would make a museum very happy.

You will need time or familiarity with the collections to ensure any effort you expend tracking down such options is well spent.

Action Step:

Although articles abound suggesting that your household possessions contain numerous valuables, consider many collections as chrome plastic, Keep a few pieces from a collection that have high sentimental value or for which you have a story. Give away the rest.

Process: Photograph the entire collection before separating pieces. As time permits, photograph individual items so you can remember them separately. Reference the chapter *PRESERVE: Digitize Your Family History* to get tips on photographing collections.

Keep: If you are downsizing your personal collection, pick your 5-7 pieces (ten if you must) of your favorite items to keep.

Give Away (Option 1): Depending upon the collection, seek out collectors or museums that would welcome your collection. Investigate the possibility of selling or transferring ownership of the pieces.

Give Away (Option 2): If you have items your children or grand-children could enjoy playing with, let them have at it. My Little Ponies benefited no one stuck in a dark, humid attic, but our children have played with them and another generation was made happy.

Give Away (Option 3): Some collections might benefit a charitable donation center. Be warned. Many donation centers have restrictions against certain items, particularly stuffed animals.

Trash: Some collections really have lost their value and should find their way to the dumpster. If you photograph it beforehand, you can do this without guilt.

Keepsakes

The value of a childhood keepsake depends upon what it is and who it belonged to. Many families save baby clothes, toys, artwork, stickers, rocks, field day t-shirts, and more. Most of these items are chrome plastic. As we age, we save even more things from our travels, activities, and occupations. Many keepsakes lose their value over time.

Action Step:

The simple action plan for keepsakes involves photographing the object and giving it a new home. In rare cases, some vintage childhood items may be donated to a historical museum or sold to a collector. Only proceed down this path if you have the time to locate a new home for such items.

Process: Digitize and discard your keepsakes. Some keepsake items fall into a document or book category (i.e., report cards, transcripts, and yearbooks, journals), place those items into the genealogical paper or book piles and evaluate them following the applicable standards discussed in later chapters.

Keep: If you have something that DEFINES your childhood or your adult life and you are willing to showcase it in your home so you can view it often, or dig it out for special occasions, then keep it.

Give Away: Consider giving items to your children or grand-children for their imaginative play.

Trash: Some keepsakes are really trash. Toss them out.

What about...?

Workshop attendees generally ask for more clarification on keepsakes, including the following:

Buggy and crib that belonged to my parents (c. 1930 - 1939) – As sweet as the memory is, this is chrome plastic. Photograph it. Then use it or give it away.

Old baseball mitt, Red Flyer sled, baby toys, father's childhood toys – Photograph these childhood treasures. Then given them away.

Dried flowers from my wedding, keepsakes from parent's mission, souvenirs from international trips – Digitize and discard many of these items. It may seem like a betrayal of some kind, but when you are downsizing, you do not have time for guilt.

Military flag from father's coffin – Many families treasure these flags. When you want to part with the flag, call your family members to discover who would like to inherit it. Gift it to them now.

Remnants of Civil War Flag my ancestor carried – This artifact might serve your family best in a museum or archive. If you do not have room to display in your home, give it to an interested family member or donate it to a museum.

Patches and Pins

Individuals receive patches and pins from their employment or vocational activities. These items tangibly depict an individual's life. However, not every patch or pin should remain in your possession when you must downsize.

I had a Math Olympiad patch from my middle school grades. Someone could suggest keeping the small patch since it consumes such little space. Small patches and pins accumulate and morph into an overwhelming avalanche. When culled to the most meaningful pieces, they are worth keeping.

I inherited some military pins that belonged to my grandfather who served in World War II. He passed away long ago, and the collection is small. I could have kept them; however, my cousin served in the military and appreciated them more. He now has those medals on display in his home.

A workshop attendee had a leather patch from the Cowboy Hall of Fame with their grandfather's name on it. Since this patch was a commemorative item and she knows the story behind it, she should keep it in the family. Otherwise, she should consider donating the patch to a rodeo or a local history museum.

Action Step:

Consider giving your pins and patches to those who would appreciate them more. Always photograph them before you give them away first.

Keep: Only the best and most beloved pieces that you are willing to hang on the wall or wear on a hat or clothing.

Process: Photograph the patches and lapel pins.

Give Away: Give historically significant patches and pins to appreciative family members.

Give Away: Donate historically significant patches and pins to museums, libraries, or archives.

Trash: If time is short, keep 3-4 beloved pieces and trash the rest.

Trophies & Medals

If you or a relative participated in any competitive activity from sports, to band, to pageants and the like, then trophies and medals are among your possessions. How do you decide what is gold and what is chrome plastic? (Most trophy's are literally chrome plastic.)

I never won Miss America or even Miss Texas. If I had, then the crown and trophy would obviously be worth keeping. I did win the titles of Miss San Jacinto Teen USA and Miss Palestine. Our family feels these crowns are gold, especially since I recorded the story of my participation in those programs. Without the story, family members can rightfully decide the tiaras are chrome plastic and give them away.

Medals do not have to come from the Olympics for your family to value them as worth keeping. You might save a 4th place ribbon from a college national baseball championship so long as you have recorded the story behind the award.

Many trophies and medals just mentioned highlight the top of a person's participation. What about the awards along the journey? How about Little League trophies or vocal competitions from elementary school? Photograph the trophies and medals received along someone's journey through their interests and career. Then discard them.

Some universities, colleges, and museums might welcome specific trophies and medals, though the chances are small unless you have items from a significant historical moment or famous athlete.

Action Step:

Photograph the ribbons, medals, and trophies before you place the items in the garbage can. You will rarely find a place that will accept these items.

Keep: The 'big victory' or triumph trophies and medals for the individuals from your family you have decided to curate, so long as you have the story behind these items.

Trash: Discard every other trophy, medal, or ribbon.

Children's Artwork

Children create so much artwork. While precious when first created, the art becomes clearly chrome plastic within a few years.

Occasionally children create stunning art pieces worth keeping. Our niece painted a pair of ballet pointe slippers. It is museum quality. This piece is gold, but any previous variations of the project should be discarded.

If you have artistic children, keep the award-winning pieces or find new homes worthy of their creativity. Otherwise, photograph and discard the art.

Action Step:

The determination of art is subjective. Ignore the nostalgia when determining the worth of a piece.

Keep: Only the best and most treasured pieces that you are willing to hang on the wall.

Process: If time permits, scan or photograph artwork and then discard the items.

Trash: If time is short, keep 3-4 beloved pieces and trash the rest.

Set Aside Your Family History As You Sift Household Items

As you reduce your household items, you will uncover documents, photos, and media of genealogical and historical significance. Set them in one central location as you empty out closets, attics, furniture, garages, storage units, file cabinets, bookcases, and boxes.

Once you have downsized your furnishings, clothing, and lifestyle items, you can sit down and prepare to tackle items of family history significance.

REDUCE: Evaluate Your Papers and Documents

Once you have processed the large items in your home: furnishings, decor, clothing, personal effects, lifestyle items, and clutter, then you can begin downsizing the areas that require the most fine-tuning and decision making.

We'll start with your papers and documents. Remember each type of paper or document will be sorted into four piles:

Keep – These are your family history gold.

Process – Mostly chrome plastic disguised as gold.

Give Away – Gold to someone else.

Trash – Chrome plastic

You'll find joy in the number of boxes, drawers, and filing cabinets you empty as you sift the priceless papers and documents from the clutter.

Know Your Family Before You Begin

Before you begin, create a list of your family surnames. You can then reference this chart when you need to determine what to keep and what to toss. A link to the Downsizing Quick Guides can be found in the *Action Plans* chapter. This includes a blank version of the surname table we use, but you can create one yourself if you want by hand or using a spreadsheet or word processor.

SURNAME TABLE				
GP	Lee	Brewer	Kevern	Tame

Row One: Working from left to right across the arc of a fan chart or from top to bottom on a pedigree chart, add the surnames of your four grandparents from left to the right on your table. The first two columns are the paternal grandparents. The last two columns are the maternal grandparents.

SURNAME TABLE				
GP	Lee	Brewer	Kevern	Tame
1st GGP	Greene	Bell	Quick	Orton

Row Two: After the four grandparent generations, you'll only add the female surnames for each generation to your chart. Thus, in the **1st GGP** row, you'll include the surnames of the females that created children with the males in the **GP** row.

SURNAME TABLE				
GP	Lee	Brewer	Kevern	Tame
1st GGP	Greene	Bell	Quick	Orton
2nd GGP	Locknane	Stevens	Tripcony	Turpin
	Harper	Shurtleff	Marte	Simpson

Row Three: Add the next generation of surnames. As you read the chart, you'll notice that the first **2nd GGP** surname (Lockname) married **GP** (Lee) and the second **2nd GGP** (Harper) married the **1st GGP** (Greene).

You can continue building this table out to as many generations as you like, but for most downsizing situations, 3 generations is enough to identify the information you need.

Pick Your Lines

In the surname table above, you have 16 family lines. Determine which family lines you wish to continue maintaining files for.

If you have limited space, you'll likely want to retain the surnames for lines you currently research. As you sort through your collection, set aside materials about lines you no longer wish to research into your process or give away piles.

Action Step:

With a clearly defined focus on pre-selected family lines, you can tackle the genealogically relevant papers and documents.

Keep: The materials for the surnames you actively research.

Give Away: Place all other materials in your giveaway pile, even if the surname appears on your surname table. In the chapter *RECLAIM: Gain Space by Giving Away*, we'll provide some suggestions as to where you might be able to donate these items.

Research of "Non-Family" or "Removed" Lines

Sometimes individuals have photos, documents, research, or artifacts that belong to friends, neighbors, associates, and in-laws. Sometimes you may discover client work or abandoned research lines. When downsizing, consider these materials as chrome plastic, that may be gold to someone else.

You might also have items from indirect paternal lines from the 3rd generation (in other words, parents of the spouses of siblings to the direct ancestors listed on your surname table). These items will definitely be gold to a direct line descendant rather than in your archive.

Action Step:

Give Away: Place all organized non-family or indirect family line documents into your giveaway pile. Review the *RECLAIM: Gain Space by Giving Away* chapter for suggestions as to where you will donate these items.

Loose Papers, Folders, Books of Remembrances, and Binders

Many people have piles of loose papers around their home. Donation centers and family members often do not accept disorganized paper stacks. When it's time to downsize, you need to reduce the piles and eventually organize the papers to increase their value to others.

Filing systems benefited individuals who wanted to organize with files rather than piles. Unfortunately, when multiple filing cabinets overflowing with papers clutter a home, this daunting downsizing challenge scares away the faint of heart.

Books of Remembrances were once a common way to contain all of your family's research. In the modern day, online databases have replaced the books, thereby condensing family history collections.

Binder organization seems unique to genealogy. It stems from the need to prove familial lines through reports and documentation. Binders may look lovely with each surname on the spine, but they consume a tremendous amount of shelf space.

Upon closer examination of the piles, files, books, and binders, you will discover an excessive amount of duplicate or unnecessary documents mixed in with the genealogy gold. Once these chrome plastic papers are removed, a manageable amount of family history remains.

Action Step:

Despite the excessive footprint these binders and files create, you may cry 10,000 rivers if you have to toss these organizational efforts in the trash. Consider giving away the files and binders to preserve your research efforts.

Give Away: Some historical and genealogical societies may accept your organized file folders and binders. Read chapter nine for more details.

You may discover a relative who appreciates and has room for your family records collection, or at least portions of it.

If you can not find a recipient for your files, books, and binders, you have to reduce your collections to save space and preserve the gold.

Golden Genealogical Documents

Genealogists find high-value records in courthouses, churches, newspapers, and archives. When you find original copies of relevant genealogy documents, then you have pure family history gold. You will easily recognize original records because of their size and paper material. Original records do not typically appear on 8.5x11 white copy paper.

In a few instances, photocopies of particular records are also gold because of the difficulty in accessing the original documents. We call these records 'near-original' because a photocopy preserves the vital information that a genealogist gleans from an original document.

```
                    GOLD PAPERS
        Any document that is an original or near-
           original for surnames you wish to
                  preserve personally.
```

Near-original records include court documents (divorce, adoption, land purchase, probate, and criminal cases) and church records (baptism, confirmation, priesthood ordination, and other religious rites). Copies of diaries, letters and family bibles also fall into this category, especially when the original source may no longer exist.

If you find any of the following items in your piles, files, books or binders, you have genealogy gold, so long as the records apply to the surnames for which you want to maintain.

- Adoption records
- Church records
- Court cases (criminal and civil)
- Divorce records
- Family Bibles
- Fraternal membership papers

- Land records
- Military discharge papers
- Naturalization applications and certificates
- Newspaper clippings
- Pension records
- Probate records
- Programs for ceremonies: weddings, funeral, baptism, inductions
- School records (award certificates, report cards, transcripts, high school diplomas)
- Wills
- Vital records (Originals Only): birth, marriage, and death records

Action Step:

While sorting your papers and documents, sort each piece into original/near-original and copies. Set the photocopies aside for now. For your original and near-original items:

Keep: Original and near-original documents that pertain to the surnames you wish to maintain or current research projects.

Give Away: Donate or give organized original and near-original records of surnames you do not wish to maintain to relatives or genealogical libraries and archives.

You will quickly separate the valuable documents from loose piles. Extracting the gold from files, books, and binders seems wrong, Why undo what someone worked so hard to do (or that you did)?

Separating gold from chrome plastic saves space. Organizing the remaining files increases the chances that your family members will preserve the downsized collection. When guilty feelings rise, set them aside. Your mission involves reducing with family history in mind and clearing out the chrome plastic achieves this objective.

Chrome Plastic Genealogical Documents

Chrome plastic genealogical papers and files refer to any photocopy of any document easily accessible online. You will recognize chrome plastic rapidly when you notice the same record copied into multiple folders or binders.

A sampling of chrome plastic documents include:

- Copies of census records
- Copies of gravestone images
- Copies of pages from published family histories
- Copies of vital records (birth, marriage, and death)
- Copies of WWI and WWII draft records
- Printouts of online gravestone memorial pages (such as Find A Grave or Billiongraves)
- Printouts of city directories
- Printouts of passenger lists

You can readily access many of these documents and more online through a free or subscription genealogy services. Many state and national archives have posted digitized originals of these documents online.

> ### CHROME PLASTIC PAPERS
> Any document or chart that can easily be reproduced from online or digitized sources.

If you are the creator of the document piles, swallow the hard truth and recognize that much of what you have gathered falls into the chrome plastic category ... thanks to online genealogy. The papers served a purpose once, but now consume too much space and obscure the gold. Remember, if your family members are not interested in genealogy, they are not going to be interested in dealing with your piles of papers. You need to deal with them now.

If you inherited genealogy or must clean out the genealogy files compiled by a loved one, most of what you have is chrome plastic. Cautiously and ruthlessly cull the collection. When you notice multiple copies of the same document, place the best one in the process pile.

Action Step:

When you discover copies while sorting, pull them out of the piles, files, books, and binders and do the following:

Keep: Keep papers only if you are currently working on a genealogy mystery or brick wall. Once you solve that research question, this information should be put into an online tree, and the printouts and photocopies can be shredded and leave your home.

Process: If you doubt whether it's accessible online, set the papers aside and process at a later date.

Trash: Any document that can be easily replaced by accessing through state archive digital collections or genealogy sites, such as Ancestry and FamilySearch, should be discarded with great haste.

Letters and Correspondence

Not all correspondence has equal value. Family members often treasure love letters because they reveal how couples met, fell in love, and the trials they faced during their courtship and marriage. Love letters fall into the family history gold category.

War letters written home to family members may also fall into the gold category. They may detail battles, struggles with unit members, or worries and instructions for the family on the home front. Find the best way to preserve these letters.

History relies on letters that contain philosophical discourses. Political rivals Thomas Jefferson and James Madison developed a strong friendship through their correspondence which discussed theories on managing the country. These letters have profound wisdom for historians, and genealogists to appreciate. If you have notes that have similar types of discussions, an archive may consider them extremely valuable.

Letters to the old country may contain genealogical clues. They often included names of family members or countrymen that help you piece together family relationships and find additional documents, such as passenger lists or naturalization papers.

However, some letters and correspondence should find their way into the trash heap. They often offer little value for the amount of space they consume.

Action Step:

Few people have the time to process an extensive correspondence collection. Ideally, you'll want to do the following:

Keep: If you know the content and context of the letters, keep them. Also, keep correspondence mentioning the surnames you decided to maintain.

Give Away: University archives, state archives, and historical societies may welcome letters of historical significance or feature prominent members of a community. If you have the time to track down a welcoming recipient, set your letter collection aside.

Give Away: A fellow genealogist may appreciate letters featuring surnames you no longer wish to maintain. Consider finding such a relative and passing the items on to them.

Trash: Letters that provide little insight into your relative's lives.

If you lack time to process a letter collection, you have a tough decision to make. Consider outsourcing the reading task to a family member who is on bed rest, an empty nester, or has a love of reading old letters. Let them review and catalog the correspondence so you can make a decision at a later date. If that is not possible, grab a box of tissues and start tossing the letters in the trash.

Diaries / Journals:

Having the thoughts and accounts of the daily life of our ancestors written in their own handwriting helps us understand their character and how they viewed the world. Many diaries seem like time machines to a specific place and time and provide a better understanding of the past. Consider journals as genealogical and historical gold; however, not all gold should reside in your home.

I had a journal that belonged to Marion Mulford of Richland County, Ohio. Marion is the ancestor of my great uncle's wife. In short, I did not want to maintain the records from this surname. This journal became chrome plastic in my hands.

I donated this diary to the Ohio History Connection archive. The archive accepted the journal because I provided pertinent facts about Marion and his connection to Ohio. A staff member read and cataloged the contents of the journal and determined it contained valuable information about Huron County in and around the Civil War. Any researcher can now access the journal via the Ohio History Connection facility in Columbus, Ohio.

Action Step:

Diaries and journals retain their value when in the correct archive.

Keep: Whenever possible, keep the diaries and journals for closely related ancestors.

Give Away: Donate journals and diaries of distant relatives to other relatives or archives and repositories.

Paper Charts

Although this section easily fits in the section on papers, folders, books, and binders section, we want to emphasize this one because many people do not view paper family trees in the document category. In workshops we have done, they will repeatedly ask what to do about the handwritten charts.

Brace yourself. Pedigree charts, family trees, and group sheets are chrome plastic. This statement generates the most considerable ire and controversy in our workshops. Surely we can not mean that the family history charts that our ancestors have handed down for generations have no value.

Yes, we do in 99.9% of cases.

Many paper charts have no supporting evidence to prove the claims on the paper. As such, a significant number of the pedigree charts and group sheets contain errors and outright fabrications. Yet, folks hold onto these inaccurate trees as if their life depends on them. "Surely Aunt Ethel didn't dare make a mistake," you may say. In actuality, she may have lacked the correct answers or lied. You never know.

Since our ancestors did not have computers, they could not pass on the family facts in an easily shareable and manageable format. Since the 1990s, many families have converted paper charts to digital trees and updated these files with accurate facts and corrections based on proper genealogical sources. In most cases, you will find an updated version of your paper charts.

Action Step:

Trash the charts!

Process: If you or your relative have not taken the time to input your tree information into a digital tree and the tree has supporting documentation, you can hold onto your charts to process later.

Trash: If your paper charts, or those of your relative's trees, have no evidence to support the statements on the paper, then discard the charts. Don't balk at this suggestion. You lack the time necessary to deal with undocumented trees.

Research Notebooks, Notes, and Logs

While we have your hackles raised, it is time to address research notebooks, notes, and logs. My mother had notebooks full of extracted information from census records, IGI files, and other resources. She wrote down the names of everyone with the Geiszler surname, in that record set in that particular place, with the intent of researching everyone to evaluate possible family connections. Additionally, she logged conversations and had loose notes aplenty. However, her notes only made sense to her.

These research notebooks served a purpose then, but computers and databases enable easier manipulation and analysis of such data today.

Action Step:

With downsizing as the goal, notes and logs consume too much space.

Trash: When you have a short timeline to downsize and have to process notebooks which do not belong to you, toss these chrome plastic items into the recycling bin. Ignore the voice that screams, "How dare you!" Shout back, "if the information had such value, the creator would have processed it before I had to make this decision."

Process: If you have a longer timeline to process the notebooks or if you created them, set aside the ones you actively use. You will need to extract the relevant information and add it to a genealogy software program. These programs have organized Research To Do List. Correspondence Logs, etc. Do yourself, and others, a favor and make use of technology for these notes so you can then embrace the trash can and toss the rest out.

Drafts of Writing Projects

Family history preserved in books have a higher chance of staying in the family for generations to come. I have a book about a great uncle named Abram Moot, which has a publication date of 1970. Published family histories may fall into the genealogical gold category. Manuscripts of unpublished books should receive careful scrutiny.

Many writers keep their first, second, and third drafts of their manuscripts. Consider only the most recent, or better yet, the published book, as worth preserving.

Action Step:

Published projects always trump drafts for said writings. Unpublished manuscripts need a path to completion. With those two points in mind, sorting previous revisions becomes easy.

Trash: When you come across your own drafts or notes for any writing that you have published in a journal or book format, give them a one-way ticket to the trash bin.

Give Away: If you lack time to prepare unpublished manuscripts for printing, then find a relative willing to receive these writings to finish the job.

Process: If you have the time and desire to finish writing the project, keep only the most current draft. Then complete it or hire someone to prepare the manuscript for publication.

Seminar Handouts and Syllabus

The most straightforward papers to downsize are seminar handout. Handouts lose their value if you do not understand the topic or did not hear the lecturer. Even then, many syllabi have lost their value as technology has changed.

Action Step:

Trash: When sorting through a loved one's files, recycle any handouts from any lectures or workshops without reading them.

If you have any handout and you don't immediately remember why you kept it, it also goes in the trash, no matter how recent.

If you attended the workshop or class, 5, 10, or 15 years ago, discard these papers in the recycling bin.

Process: Keep handouts from recent seminars if you have consulted it regularly since the workshop.

Business Files

Business files may reveal the nature of a family and their relationship to other community members. Some historic business files have enabled researchers to find their missing family members, including females who may not show up in other records. However, not every paper that pertains to a business retains its value over time. Many business files were created to be disposable and should be discarded. Some document must be retained for tax purposes, but once you have processed them, shred them.

Consider legal papers defining the scope and location of the business or historic ledgers detailing daily transactions with specific individuals as gold. A friend had the store ledger that accounted for every transaction their family farm conducted from 1840 - 1900. The changes of handwriting and the scope of the family farm provides the context of her ancestor's livelihood in rural Iowa. For her, this item contains genealogical gold.

In contrast, I worked at a used car dealership as a teenager. That business generated thousands of pounds of paper every year through inventorying cars, issuing and managing loans, paying employees, recording repair work, and filing for repossession. Many of those files sat in deep storage after the tax requirement for holding such papers expired. If we inherited said business files today, most of them would go into an industrial shredder.

The following items have value for family history purposes:

- Tax ID certificates for the operation of the business
- Samples of advertisements the company ran
- Logos or small business iconography
- Newspaper clippings about the business owner and his/her contribution to the community
- Photos of the business office, location, and employees overtime
- Scrapbooks that feature the history of the business
- Ledger books

Action Step:

If you encounter business files in your family archive or your home, quickly process the collection

Keep: Items for businesses your close relations owned that appear on the above list.

Give Away: Some archives and repositories collect historic business files.

Trash: The remaining business files should be discarded.

Celebrate the Reduction of the Paper Files

When you have sifted out the gold from the chrome plastic, the valuable from the clutter, your paper collection may decrease as much as 75-80%. Even with that volume of paper reduction, you still may have a sizable collection of high-value genealogical documents that future family historians will love and appreciate.

You can downsize the papers and documents and preserve your legacy. The Downsizing Quick Guides (link can be found in the *Action Plans* chapter at the end of this book) includes a Quick Guide to Evaluating Papers and Photos which you can use during your downsizing.

REDUCE: Evaluate Your Books and Periodicals

Genealogists hoard books like squirrels store nuts. When it's time to downsize, books have overstayed their welcome. When home libraries decrease to a few modest bookshelves, many individuals are astonished by the amount of free floor and shelf space that remains.

Review the chapter *REDUCE: Evaluate Your Household Items*, specifically the section regarding collections and clutter for tips on reducing general interest books. For books relevant to genealogy and your family legacy, this chapter adds more insights. For the most part, bid farewell to most books, even if you shed tears as you do.

Remember each book or periodical will be sorted into one of four piles:

Keep – These are your family history gold.

Process – Mostly chrome plastic disguised as gold.

Give Away – Gold to someone else.

Trash – Chrome plastic.

If you successfully reduce your general household items following guidelines from the previous chapter, you will find joy witnessing the number of boxes and shelves cleared by these tips.

Family Bibles

Many people consider Family Bibles as invaluable treasures. Many such Bibles pre-date civil registrations and therefore provide the only source of your ancestor's birth, marriage, and death dates. In most cases, we recommend that you keep the Family

Bible! You should also consider buying a storage box specifically designed to preserve old books, to store your Family Bible in.

Yet, not all Family Bibles have the same value. Some bibles served as study guides. Owners highlighted favorite passages, recorded thoughts and impressions, and dog-eared corners. These notations provide glimpses into the faith of your Bible owner. If you can identify the individual who made the notes, you may have gold. You should keep the Bible if the original owner falls into the surnames for which you wish to continue serving as family archivist. Otherwise, the Bible has become clutter, and you should find it a new home.

Action Step:

Family Bibles often have genealogical and personal history gold inside, but only if the book belongs to the family lines, you want to retain personally.

Keep: Family bibles that have genealogical data or defined family history connections if they are on your chosen list of surnames to curate.

Give Away (Option 1): Donate historical Bibles such as first editions or Bibles used by historical figures, to museums and repositories.

Give Away (Option 2): Donate a Bible that does not contain genealogical information or lacks markings by an ancestor for use by missions and other charitable groups.

For Family Bibles you do retain, identify the person who will inherit these books when you pass away. Choose someone who will recognize the value of the Family Bible. If no such person exists, find repositories or archives that will gladly accept the Bibles. Then make plans in your will for those facilities to receive the Bibles upon your death.

In addition to sorting which Family Bibles to keep, you should purchase an appropriate archival quality storage box for each book. Finally, plan on digitizing the genealogical information in each Bible.

Story-Based Published Family Histories

Not every published family history has equal worth. Bound family histories filled with numerous stories and photos provide a portal to the past. Published family histories may contain short stories, a collection of biographical essays, a recipe book with family history inside, a scrapbook with images and text, or a generational book with biographies of an ancestor (or couple) and then a listing of their descendants.

However, if the published family history contains little besides family group sheets and pedigree charts, the content has lost its worth. Read the next section for what to do about these books.

Action Step:

If you have books that bring your ancestors to life through narration rather than charts, you have gold, even if the books focus on distant relatives.

Keep: As much as possible, keep the story-centric family histories.

Process: Search the online catalogs of archives and/or libraries to ensure that a copy of the book is accessible to other family researchers.

Give Away: Donate books about distant relations that you don't have room to keep to a researcher more closely related to the subject or to an archive or applicable genealogy society that does not have the book in its holdings.

Chart Heavy Published Family History Books

In the past, many families published nothing more than family relationship reports and pedigree charts in bound books. Before the digital revolution and the age of online genealogy, these printed publications were useful. Most such family histories have online versions with more up-to-date research and corrections. Additionally, digital versions of many printed family histories appear in internet book archives.

Action Step:

If you flip through a printed family history and more than 70% of its pages have reproduced charts or brief facts about who married whom, then you have chrome plastic.

Process: If the published book contains sources, then search the WorldCat website or a library catalog for the family history. Search the Internet Archive, Google Books, FamilySearch Books, Ancestry, or Hathi Trust and other similar sites for your published family history. Discard books that appear in these collections.

Give Away: Donate the sourced publish family history to a genealogical society or library in the area the families lived.

Trash: Trash any chart book that lacks supporting evidence

Research Guides And Reference Books

Research guides assist genealogists in conducting research and include such titles as *Finding Vital Records Research Guide, Finding U.S. Naturalization Records, Tracing Irish Ancestors Online*, and *New York Family History Guide and Gazetteer*. Generally, reference books offer little more than an index to something such as "Burials in St. Mary's Catholic Cemetery, Alexandria, Virginia, 1798-1983", "Burke County, North Carolina, Marriage Record Index,1781-1868", and "California Pioneer Register and Index."

In most cases, researchers can access both the research guides and reference books at libraries and archives or through online sources. Many such books have ebook versions for easier access.

Since libraries, digital archives, and online databases have superseded many references books, discard them without guilt. Do not waste your valuable time attempting to donate them to others.

Action Step:

When you are downsizing, ruthlessly decrease your collection of research guides and reference books.

Process: Keep only the guides and books relevant to your current research and projects.

Trash: Drop any book or guide for topics you do not frequently reference into the recycling bin.

Methodology Books

If the content of a genealogy book begins with, "fill out a group sheet, write letters to archives, or search through microfilm or CD-ROMs," then recycle the book based on its outdated content. The amount of relevant information in such books is so minute that the recycled paper industry would welcome your contribution.

Modern methodology books might start with completing a group sheet, but most should have a substantial amount of online research strategies and tree building. With that said, online genealogy rapidly changes. Most genealogy books printed in the 2000s contain suggestions to visit websites and resources that no longer exist. Many of the links no longer work for companies and organizations still in existence.

Take for example my book *Power Scrapbooking: Getting Caught Up No Matter Your Scrapbook Style* written 9 years ago. The programs and digital recommendations from that book are no longer valid because of the enormous decrease in resources in the digital scrapbooking industry. I released a second edition that's now entitled *Power Scrapbooking* and expect it to be obsolete in about 4 years.

Many methodology books, even outdated content, appear on the shelves of public libraries. Many have ebook versions available for purchase or loan. Therefore, do not bother donating such books to libraries, societies, or archives.

Action Step:

When it comes to methodology books, ruthlessly cull your collection to make room for the family history that matters most.

Trash: Discard outdated methodology books because they have lost their value.

Keep: If you are downsizing your genealogy methodology book collection, only keep those books you consider to be Genealogy Bibles, and you consult them frequently.

History Books

Some genealogists collect history books to understand better the context in which their ancestors lived. Though these books provide historical context for genealogists, they have no value in a home facing downsizing.

The Lee Family bookshelves are full of history books for our children to teach them about Benjamin Franklin, Harriet Tubman, and the bombing of Pearl Harbor. These books only have value so long as our children live in our home.

Publishers mass produced history books. Libraries utilize the interlibrary loan system to share publications with their patrons, decreasing the need to have numerous copies in circulation and consuming shelf space. Therefore, when you reduce your historical book collection, treat them like romance novels and drop them off at a book sale or in the recycling bin.

Action Step:

For history books, you will likely have one action to take.

Trash: Discard the history books in the collection.

What about rare books?

Just because a book is old does not mean it's valuable. If you have 12 months to downsize and you know the value of a book, you can spend time trying to find a new home for it. If the value is questionable, do not sacrifice time better spent preserving family history gold by holding on to old books of dubious value.

City Directories, County Histories, and Yearbooks

Depending upon your level of pack-rat addiction, you might have some gold in your home that is coveted by genealogists around the world. These golden books include city directories, county histories, and yearbooks.

City directories resemble phone books, but without phone numbers. They began in the early 1700s and were printed until the early 1900s when they were replaced by phone books. City directories rarely turn up outside of an archive. If you do discover one in fair to good condition, you should investigate whether an online copy exists and whether there is an online repository that would accept it.

County histories recorded the lives of early settlers to an area or were created in celebration of historical anniversaries. Genealogists access most county histories through library collections or digital archives. If you have a county history in your collection, investigate whether or not a copy appears in WorldCat, a digital archive, or in a county-specific historical or genealogical society.

Yearbooks (the older, the better) cover primary, secondary, and collegiate level education. They may contain the only photos of an ancestor that exist today. Additionally, they may reveal the activities an ancestor participated in while obtaining their education. Many yearbooks in decent condition from the 1800s and early 1900s are highly sought after. Spend time investigating whether a copy of the yearbook appears in libraries or archives that serve the area featured in the yearbook. Or search websites that have digital yearbook collections, such as Ancestry or MyHeritage, for the edition you have.

Of the three books listed in this section, only yearbooks should warrant the consideration of remaining in your archive if they feature the surnames about which you have chosen to curate.

Action Step:

City directories, county histories, and yearbooks contain valuable information for a large number of family historians. Whenever possible, take time to find the best homes for these books.

Give Away: Investigate whether the city directories, county histories, and yearbooks appear in the collections for a society, library, or archive that serves the location features in these books. If these repositories lack the books you have, donate the books to them.

Keep: Save yearbooks that belong to family relations that you chose to keep in your archive.

Trash: County histories or city directories that are in disrepair. Any of the three types of books that have duplicate copies in libraries, archives, or online collections.

Magazines and Journals

Quickly decide to trash fan, trade and scholarly journals and magazines. To preserve the personal interests of yourself or that of a loved one who owned the collection, take a few pictures of the entire collection. Then grab the dust collecting printed material and drop it in the recycling bin.

Most libraries and some digital archives have copies of the printed material you will handle while downsizing. If you have regional specific content and the time to investigate, you could search repositories to ensure they have copies of those particular magazines and journals.

If this is your periodical collection and you remember specific articles that you wish to keep for an active research project, tear out that article. Then trash the rest of the magazine or journal. Keep your clipping pile VERY, VERY small and don't spend too much time hunting for the article you need.

Action Step:

Don't spend your time sifting through these low-value items. Place them in a recycling bin without guilt.

Process: To preserve the personal interests of the collection owner, photograph the entire collection then the front covers of a few issues.

Give Away: If you discover magazines that are more than 30 years old and feature a historical event, consider listing the items on eBay or find a history museum or archive interested in the magazine. (Only if you have the time and resources to do so).

Trash: Discard fan, trade, and scholarly magazines and journals.

Celebrate Your Smaller Library

Books and periodicals can take up substantial amounts of floor and shelf space. This chapter provided straightforward principles on what to Keep, Process, Give Away, and Trash.

Do not allow a large bookcase, which needs to be downsized, intimidate you. Use the guidelines in this chapter to efficiently reduce a book and periodical collection in under an hour. All that remains could amount to a handful of books that will fit in your backpack or a single bookshelf.

REDUCE: Evaluate Your Photos and Media

Photos, videos, and other media generate a lot of discussion in our downsizing workshops. Do they automatically fall into the gold category? Could they mistakenly seem valuable when in actuality they should sort into the chrome plastic piles? This chapter analyzes photos and media based on several factors and assigns value accordingly.

You will ultimately sort each photo, slide, audio recording, and home movie into one of four piles:

Keep – These are your family history gold.

Process – Mostly chrome plastic disguised as gold.

Give Away – Gold to someone else.

Trash – Chrome plastic

Be warned the number one time suck during downsizing involves photos and media. People usually have thousands of pictures and movies which take time to review. Nostalgia kicks in, and we start to relive the memories attached to each photo or video.

When you are clearing out a home and have a lengthy timeline, tackle the household items, the papers and books, and then spend whatever time you have left on photos.

If you have a short amount of time to clear out a family home, grab the photos and papers before taking the household items.

Photos

In many cases, you should retain your photo collection if the individuals within pertain to the surnames you have chosen to curate. Images of our relatives, both the living and the dead, are priceless. However many pictures should be discarded. How do you tell the difference?

Before you can sort your photos, you must gather them in one location. You will find pictures around your home in three major formats:

Framed photos carry the most sentimental value and appear in a wide assortment of sizes and shapes.

Photo albums, boxes, and envelopes house a variety of photo collections. The fortunate family archivist has photo collections organized chronologically, by event, or by family.

Loose photos appear in the strangest of places such as in books, stacks of paper, boxes, cedar chests, and drawers.

Reduce your framed pictures. Most people do not have room for an extensive collection of framed photos in their downsized living spaces. Additionally, descendants rarely want framed images, preferring updated styles or smaller sizes. Reduce your framed photo collection to those with the highest sentimental value that fit the available space in your new living situation.

Remove photos from the remaining frames and all albums if possible. If a photo begins to rip, then leave the pictures in place. Combine these pictures with those assembled from shoeboxes, store envelopes, and loose piles.

Arrange the images in chronological order before further evaluation of the pictures.

Action Steps:

When downsizing, plan on digitizing and discarding photos larger than 8x10 if no family members desire them.

Process: Photograph framed photos as they appear in a household before moving them. Photograph each photo album page to preserve the arrangement of images and their possible clues to one another.

Process: Corral all loose photos, frames portraits, photo albums, boxes and envelopes in one central processing location.

Trash: As you are processing the pictures, immediately discard items with mold or other hazardous materials.

How to evaluate the worth of photos

Photo collections full of clutter consume valuable space and decrease the chances the entire collection remains in the family archive. Cull the pictures to the images with the highest family history value. There are many ways we can categorize our photographs and with most of these below, the necessary actions become apparent.

Poor Quality Photos

Do not allow poor quality pictures to clutter your photo collection. Drop significantly overexposed or underexposed images and blurry subjects straight in the trash bin.

Action Steps:

Trash: Discard poor quality images.

Inappropriate Photos

Remove inappropriate photos from your photo collection. Photos of offensive or crude imagery should not overwhelm your family history. Save a few images to preserve an accurate glimpse into the past, but not all of them.

Action Steps:

Do not clutter your photo collection with too many inappropriate images.

Keep: A few photos if you wish to preserve an accurate picture of the past.

Give Away: Some museums and archives will accept questionable images for their historical collection to accurately depict the past. Consider donating the pictures if you feel they can add to the collective history of a topic.

Trash: Discard inappropriate or offensive images.

Damaged Photos

Many old pictures have tears, stains, or faded colors. Restoring damaged photos may become time-consuming or costly. Only keep the most valuable images for restoration work. Remove other significantly damaged photos from your collection.

Action Step:

Do not let significantly damaged images mar your photo collection.

Keep: If a photo has a minor flaw or discoloration, leave it in your collection as is. The flaws tell a story as much as the actual image does.

Process: If a photo has significant flaws you will repair, set them aside for that purpose.

Trash: Discard photos that are damaged beyond repair.

Duplicate Photos

Duplicate photos bloat many photo collections. This often happened when individuals purchased family and school portraits packages. You only need to retain one copy of the school or family picture. Opt to keep portraits sized 8x10 or a smaller sized image.

In the days when ordering double prints from the photo lab became the norm, our photo collections ballooned as well. Reduce the picture stockpile to one representation of the moment.

Some collections have multiple similar pictures because a photographer hoped one would turn out well. Reduce the apparent duplicates from your collection before digitizing or organizing the remaining prints.

Action Step:

Do not let duplicate images bloat your photo collection.

Give Away: Ask family members if they want any of the dupli-cate copies of the photo collection, then give the prints to them.

Trash: Discard any leftover duplicates.

Unlabeled Photos

If your photo collection indicates names of the people, the date the taken, and what was going on in the photo either on the back of the picture or surrounding the image in a photo album, then you may have gold. Then again, you have to ensure you only keep pictures for the surnames you decided to curate.

What photos you keep depends on the amount of time you have to process the pictures. If you have a limited amount of time to reduce a household, cull the collection to the photographs with identifying information. Toss out the unidentified portraits.

Case in point, when my mother died, I only had a few days to sort a 3-foot stack of photo albums. I ruthlessly tossed the uniden-tified photos. I could not justify the cost of transporting 15 photo albums of unnamed friends, neighbors, and church associates from my parents' many moves through the 1970s and 1980s. How-ever, I did save every photo and scrapbook page that had pictures of identified individuals or those I recognized.

Do I feel guilty? While I discarded the unlabeled photos, my genealogy heart broke. I know the value of keeping pictures. However, since my parents did not take the time to identify the people and places, the remaining images held no meaning. As such, the guilt has lessened the farther removed I have become over the past six years.

Action Step:

If a photo has no identifying information, then you have chrome plastic. Unidentified photos pepper nearly every family photo collection.

Process: If you think you can label the photos from your memory or that of a relative, keep the pictures until you can identify them.

Trash: Discard any image that remains unidentified.

Slides / Negatives

Slides and negatives create challenges because you often can not view them before you print the images. Few of us have the means to look at slides and negatives before we develop them. If possible, try to magnify the images to decide which are worth developing. Otherwise, you will either have to pay to develop the slides and negatives knowing that a significant percentage could be useless. In short, you could spend a lot of time preserving slides and negatives that you will likely discard after they are developed.

When attempting to decide which slides or negatives to develop, hold each to the light. If you can determine that the picture features people or homes then consider developing those images. If you see foliage, animals, and landscapes, then discard the slides and negatives without guilt. By processing people and homes, you will reduce the chance of printing potentially worthless images.

Action Step:

In many instances, slides and negatives have indeterminate value until you can view an enlarged copy of the image.

Give Away: If family members have the means to develop the slides and negatives, send them these items.

Trash: Discard slides and negatives if you are short on time and do not have the means to process the images.

If you have the means to digitize your slides and negatives, reduce the collection before sending them to the developer.

Process: Remove slides from carousels and trays and place them in slide storage boxes. This will quickly reduce the storage space required for your collection.

Trash: Discard slides and negatives after you have made a digital copy of the images.

Many archivists will shoot us for telling you to toss things out. Some archives will accept your slides and negatives, but the question is, "Do you have the time to find such archives and the space to store the negatives?" If you do not, then follow these action steps.

Scrapbooks

Through the decades, scrapbooks have taken on many styles. Some books contain quotes, scriptures, or favorite celebrities or news stories. Others organize photos, souvenirs, and documents. Scrapbooks regularly record the personality and character of the individual who curated the books. These treasures fall easily into the gold category.

Action Step:

Although scrapbooks provide glimpses into the past, not every scrapbook retains its value in your home:

Keep: The scrapbooks of the surnames for which you decided to be the family archivist. Place the scrapbooks in proper archival quality boxes.

Give Away (Option 1): Send photo albums to family members who will willingly preserve the scrapbooks you can no longer store.

Give Away (Option 2): If you have time and resources. Attempt to locate an archive that accepts scrapbooks you no longer wish to keep.

Process: When you have time, digitize the scrapbook to preserve the images and content.

Trash: If you must downsize quickly, then throw away scrapbooks full of unidentified individuals.

Recorded Interviews or Performances

Having an ancestor tell their stories in their own words touches the hearts of many. The stories are invaluable along with the sound of their voice. Many genealogists would donate their kidney or liver for recorded interviews.

Some families also have talented singers, musicians, dancers, actors, and the like. If your family has audio or video recordings of these performances, they will be treasured if they are preserved.

If the interviews and performances feature individuals you can no longer keep in your collection, then find someone who would love the media files. If you have an ancestor's war stories and they happen to have served in the US military, send a copy of the digital recording to the National Archives for preservation at your earliest opportunity. Many oral interviews would be welcomed by oral history projects at libraries and archives. Do not forget to investigate individuals more closely related to the subjects in the interview or performances. They might willingly accept your donation.

Action Step:

Keep: Recordings of the relatives of whom you wish to be the curator.

Process: Digitize the recordings. Edit out the fluff and dead space to reduce their storage space.

Give Away: Donate recordings to distant relatives, archives, libraries, or oral history projects.

Home Movies

The rising generations love videos. If you have home movies, plan on properly preserving and sharing this media.

Many families do not have the technology to view old movie formats such as reel to reel, 35 mm, and VHS. Many formats deteriorate over time. Plan to digitize the media to conserve space and preserve the memories.

Having edited numerous family videos, not every minute of home movies is valuable. For instance, some of my pageant tapes are 2 hours long, but I appear for perhaps 2-4 minutes in those videos. In a 10 minute clip of our children, only 1 minute has memorable moments.

Some home videos have historical significance and would enhance the special collections of archives and museums. Contact these archives to determine if they will accept movies in their traditional format. Please note that many no longer take footage that has not been converted to digital formats.

If you have movies that lack a label identifying its content, chances are the video is not valuable. Additionally, many VHS and other tapes are recordings of copy written material such as movies or television episodes. Discard these movies from your collection.

Action Step:

Home movies contain significant sentimental value. Digitize them, and you will conserve your space and preserve your family history.

Process: To properly preserve the home movies and reduce the space they consume in your home, digitize them. Also, plan on editing out the fluff and dead space.

Give Away: Donate recordings to interested distant relatives, archives, libraries, or oral history projects.

Trash: Discard unlabeled home videos or those featuring copy-written material.

Preserve the Perishable Photos and Media

Photos, audio records, and movies contain significant family history value. When digitized, these media items consume less space. You do not have to sacrifice the memories to downsize to a few framed photos and an organized photo collection. You can easily access your entire audio and visual recordings after converting them to digital formats.

If you saved the sorting of your photos and media to the last step, you can now visualize the amount of space you saved without sacrificing your family legacy. You can now focus your efforts on preserving and showcasing your family history in your down-sized living space.

Downsizing Action Plan

Why wait until the middle of a book about Downsizing to start talking about action plans? Many people don't realize the scope and magnitude that downsizing may entail so hopefully over the previous chapters you have started to get a sense of what all needs to get done. Knowing more about the scope can help you in making the plan you need to be successful.

The sooner you start downsizing, the better care your household items will receive. If you are up against the clock, you will need an action plan that will rapidly reduce your household goods while preserving some family history. In this chapter, you will find strategies if you lack sufficient time to downsize or and action plans if you have months or years to execute a plan.

Reality TV De-cluttering

If you have watched any downsizing or de-cluttering reality show, they will gather everything out of a house or a room that they plan on cleaning out and put it in one place. Those television shows imply that the homeowners sift through the massive pile of belongings in an hour.

Reality TV has very little to do with reality. It is edited for television, which means, you are not going to sort through everything in an hour. If you have a 2,000-3,000 square foot home, a garage, a barn, a workshop and so on, the 'reality show' de-cluttering pace is unrealistic.

If you have a short downsizing timeline, you will make choices rapidly as you remove furnishings and possessions from a home. Once an item leaves the door, it will go on the keep truck, in a process box, in the give away pile, or the trash can. You will not have the luxury to move things twice.

If you have a 6-12 month timeline, you can maneuver items into staging areas around your home. Perhaps one room becomes the keep area. Another room has boxes for items to process. The give away piles may find their way to one room until after a garage or estate sale or you have donated them to appropriate facilities and individuals. The trash can cart off items any time it fills and spills over.

In short, you rarely need to downsize on the front lawn.

Prepare Your Mind

Before we explore a different downsizing strategy, you have to prepare your mind. Keep the following four tips in mind when you begin downsizing:

**STOP ADDING
ANYTHING NEW**

From this moment forward, do not buy any new furnishing, collect any new genealogical document, or purchase any new products. Until you have reduced your stash, you do not need to add anything new. Do not even think of purchasing organizing containers either. In short, the only thing you should buy are household consumeables: food, medicine, toiletries, and cleaning products.

For the genealogical researcher, you may find this key difficult. You can not print off any more records, family group sheets, or other discoveries. You must save any new genealogy document to a computer filing system, in a genealogical software program or on an online tree. It might kill you to go digital, but adding new papers to your household will not help you downsize. Say no to paper genealogy.

Once you stop adding to your household, tackle the mountain and make it a molehill

START NOW

No matter your situation, you can never start too early on sorting through your belongings and eliminate anything that has lost its value or purpose.

Starting now will also spread out the emotional difficulty that arises as you begin to reminisce about the high and low moments of the past. Downsizing is a psychological roller coaster. Spreading out the hills and valleys of the ride produces less overwhelm and better decisions for the future.

Start now. The greatest gift you can give your loved ones is a downsized, well-organized household that preserves your family history.

Start now, because today is yesterday's someday.

START SMALL

Whenever possible, do not tackle an entire house in one day. Find joy in reducing one room at a time. Celebrate each time you empty out one or more boxes from your storage unit, closet, attic, or garage. Celebrate clearing off one bookshelf of a five-shelf piece. Remember to apply the moral of Aesop's fable, "Slow and steady wins the race"

Even if you have a short amount of time to clean out a home, simplify the process to one step at a time. Complete one manageable task before moving on to another.

BE CONSISTENT

When you know you have time to downsize, even if it is 3 months rather than 12, be consistent and be proactive in accomplishing your task. Letting the task wait until the last minute will create too many mistakes. You want to downsize so you can preserve what matters most.

Make a date with yourself and your downsizing project at regular intervals based on your overall timeline. Set aside several hours daily to reduce your possessions if your timeline is short. Pick one room each week of your 3-month timeline to reduce and preserve.

Spend 6 months working on reducing the paper and media files and the remaining 6 months reducing the furnishings, housewares, decor, clothing, and lifestyle items as you might be actively using them.

As you stop collecting new things, start now, start small, and be consistent, you can successfully downsize with family history in mind when you have a road map.

Action Plans Based on Time

Have you ever heard, *"Failing to plan means planning to fail"*? Many people avoid plans like the plague. Downsizing a home warrants planning.

Engineers know a lot about project management. Andy, an engineer by trade, often helps me plan out my big projects. I prefers to wing things but often wind up frustrated and inefficient. However, when Andy's plans allow for some free-spirited wiggle room, they accomplish my big ideas. Find a way to balance the outlined approach to downsizing with the free-spirited whims so that the end goal is accomplished.

Perhaps you will set up a timeline for which rooms and categories of home items to reduce, but allow for the free-spirited individual to be lost in nostalgia in a different room. Also allow for that psychological distraction. Downsizing includes hesitancy to make decisions, tears and laughter as memories resurface. Do not over schedule the process.

Real World Downsizing

To make a downsizing plan in your real world, you need to know two things:

1. How much time do you have?
2. What is the size of your downsizing project?

The action plan that you employ for a small collection with a long timeline will be vastly different than a 4 bedroom home with an attic and a week to clean out completely. There are even different action plans for individuals who will be reducing their personal possessions from a 2,000 square foot home to a 900 square foot condo.

The more time you have, the more time you can spend dealing with chrome plastic that still has value, but not to you. The less time you have, the more emphasis you are going to spend on preserving clearly defined gold items and addressing questionable chrome plastic items as time and space permits.

The following are some sample action plans to help you start to develop your own based on your situation. You can find detailed versions of these action plans at the end of this book in the *Action Plans* chapter along with a link to a file contains the Downsizing Quick Guides we have developed to help downsize. If your timeline is shorter, or longer, follow the plan with the most similar time increment.

1-Hour Action Plan:

May you never have to utilize a 1-hour action plan. Think mother died, lives in an apartment, and I have one-hour to grab the essentials. Or perhaps an evacuation of your neighborhood is mandated due to an imminent natural or manmade disaster.

If you find yourself in a quick grab situation: focus on photos, documents, and family history books. If time permits, you can grab a few trinkets and keepsakes but you need to focus on saving documents and images.

- Photograph home before downsizing begins.
- Photograph each room and the large details.
- Photograph prized collections as a whole.
- Keep photos (loose, organized, framed, albums, or envelopes).
- Keep genealogy binders, file folders, and family history books (if possible).
- Keep documents, media, and family history books.
- Keep jewelry.
- Keep a few trinkets or keepsakes.
- Give away any previously determined or specified inheritance items to heirs.

As time permits, you can keep lifestyle items, clothing and small furnishings. When the time ends, you leave the rest to work crews to donate to charity or sell as they see fit.

Weekend Action Plan:

A weekend to downsize provides a little more time for preserving family history beyond the obvious genealogy material. Give priority to photographing the living space to memorialize the home in that moment in time.

If you are downsizing yourself or a loved one to live in a new place, move furniture, furnishings, clothing, and lifestyle items that you must have for continued life in the new space. Do not take everything. Only the essential and functional items.

- Photograph home before downsizing begins.
- Photograph each room and the large details.

94

- Photograph prized collections as a whole.
- Move furnishings, clothing, and lifestyle items essential for living to new space.

When the necessities are out of the way, focus on downsizing what remains.

- Give away any previously determined or specified inheritance items to heirs.
- Rapidly sort through remaining furnishings and clothing. Keep only items that are genealogy gold.
- Give away remaining furnishings and clothing in good condition to charity collection centers.
- Trash furnishings and clothing that are broken or are unacceptable to charity collection centers (such as TVs or undergarments).

With the above removed from your decision making, tackle the collections, media, and documents. You will quickly run out of time if you let nostalgia win. Focus on speed and saving the most valuable items in the following categories. You know that if you had more time, you would salvage more items. But with a short timeline, you have to be heartless.

- Reduce prized collections to 5-10 favorite pieces.
- Give away or trash the rest of the pieces.
- Rapidly sort through photos loose, envelopes, framed, or albums for identified individuals.
- Keep only pictures that can be identified, no matter the surname.
- Trash all photos and photo albums with unidentified individuals that you do not recognize personally.
- Rapidly sort through document piles, files, and binders.
- Keep only the original documents and images.
- Keep only charts that have sources on them.

- Trash all genealogy papers that contain notes, photocopies, and family group sheets with no identified sources.
- Keep story-based family history books, home movies, slides, and negatives.
- Trash books, magazines, and movies according to Downsizing Quick Guides (link can be found in the *Action Plans* chapter at the end of this book).
- Trash remaining clutter.

After your initial downsizing, make plans to downsize your genealogy photos, slides, media, and documents further. You might have to live with boxes on your bed for a few weeks as you properly preserve these items.

Notice that the only give away piles you have are the items for previously determined or specified inheritance items to heirs and anything that a donation center will accept.

Unfortunately, in a weekend, you don't have time to contact genealogical societies, museums, and unknown distant relatives to accept anything that is chrome plastic disguised as gold.

Most individuals facing a weekend downsizing situation most likely are not reading this book. If you are reading this book and have a family member, friend, or church member who needs assistance, you are prepared with a plan that will greatly help them out. Hand them the appropriate Downsizing Quick Guides (link can be found in the *Action Plans* chapter at the end of this book) to processing papers and photos. Do not let them be sentimental unless they are willing to maintain whatever they are telling you to keep (which they also have room for).

Short timelines for downsizing must focus on saving the obvious gold. Mistakes will be made, but hopefully they will be reduced with this action plan and the guide to what is valuable from a family history perspective.

3-5 Month Action Plan:

A 3-5 month timeline is the most common situation individuals face with regard to downsizing. You have time to do more than a weekend crash course, but you can not preserve everything in the ways discussed in the evaluation chapters.

This timeline front loads processing your photos, documents, and collections. As such, you can ensure all of these items are backed up and in a new format to enjoy that takes up less space.

The 3-5 month plan might allow you to take more care with your photos. Perhaps someone in the family knows the details behind the unidentified people and places and can help you reduce your mystery photos to a very small number.

You may also have time to host a physical or online sale of your items before taking them to a charitable donation center. You will likely not have time to contact museums or collectors, unless you have connected with them previously.

With 3-5 months, you may have time to find family members interested in your genealogy files or genealogical societies and archives. Your search for such recipients will be shallow. If you can't find a person or a facility within your timeline, you have to make alternative places for your items

3-5 Months Before Downsize Deadline

- Photograph home before downsizing begins.
- Photograph each room and the large details.
- Photograph key dinnerware pieces.
- Photograph treasured clothing items individually.
- Photograph sentimental home decor items individually.

Collections:

- Photograph prized collections as a whole.
- Photograph collection items individually.
- Reduce prized collections to 5-10 favorite pieces.
- Give away collections that will be gold to someone else: Family Members, Garage / Estate Sales, Online selling sites, Charity collection centers.
- Trash the rest.

Documents:

- Give away binders and files for family lines you no longer wish to maintain to genealogy libraries or historical societies.

- Give away binders and files to family members interested in the work.

- Process the piles, files, and binders for any family line you are actively researching.

- Trash all papers that are photocopies and family group sheets with no identified sources.

- Keep original or near-original genealogical documents.

- When in doubt about the value of a paper, keep it to process later.

- Process family group sheets that have sources. Once information is in a digital tree, trash these sheets.

- Place images in the photo piles.

- Reduce the organization of the papers to the fewest files or binders as possible.

- Trash all papers that photocopies, and family group sheets on abandoned family lines.

- Trash all other papers based on the Downsizing Quick Guides (link can be found in the *Action Plans* chapter at the end of this book).

Photos:

- Trash blurry, duplicate, or inappropriate photos.

- Trash photos with an unclear or confusing purpose.

- Keep photos that are labeled.

- Process photos that are not labeled.

- Give away unidentified photos to the website Dead Fred.

- Trash all photos and photo albums with unidentified individuals that you were unable to determine in 3-5 months.

Other Media:

- Reduce collection to slides and negatives that depict people and buildings.
- Trash slides and negatives that do not meet the above standard.
- Temporarily reduce the storage containers for slides and negatives until digitization is complete.
- Process book, magazine, and movie collection by photographing the collections as a whole
- Photograph a few unique or notable items.
- Trash books, magazines, and movies.
- Keep story-based family history books and home movies.
- Trash chart based family histories.
- Keep genealogy methodology and resource books that you are actively using.
- Trash outdated genealogy methodology and resource books.

After your initial downsizing, make plans to downsize your genealogy photos, slides, media, and documents further. You should outsource the digitization of your photos, slides, negatives, and other media to a company that specializes in digitizing. These companies will be able to do the job while you are working on other downsizing tasks. Begin processing your genealogy documents to further reduce to only original and near-original papers.

1 - 2 Months Before Downsize Deadline

While you are processing the genealogically items, you slowly sort and process your furnishings, clothing, and lifestyle items. A 3-5 month timeline usually means you are living with these items as you are downsizing. Embrace the joy of having fewer items in each room.

Furnishing, Housewares, Clothing, Personal Effects:

- Give away any previously determined or specified inheritance items to heirs.

- Keep furnishings, clothing, and essential items you will move to use in the new space.
- Keep furnishings, clothing, and lifestyle items that fit in the new space and have sentimental value.
- Give away furnishings, clothing, personal effects that will be gold to someone else: Family Members, Garage / Estate Sales, charity collection centers.
- Trash large furnishings, clothing, personal effects, and home decor from the home that are broken, do not sell, or are unacceptable to charity collection centers.

12 Month Action Plan (or "I've inherited a box, or two, of my relative's stuff")

If you are looking to preserve your household goods in the most places, including collectors, museums, and archives, then your best option is to have 12 months or more to accomplish this goal. Additionally, you can reduce much of your genealogy chrome plastic by processing the documents of questionable value with the use of online trees or desktop genealogy software.

You will have the most time to process unidentified photos. If you still can not identify the individuals, you can donate them to libraries or a website like DeadFred.com. You can still have estate sales and sell your items online, but now you have more time to have multiple in-person sales or time the online sales to their best advantage.

The longer time frame allows you to take more care with your photos. You can trash the poor quality images, digitize all photos (including the mysteries), and ask for help to identify individuals that are unidentified.

12 Months Before Downsize Deadline

- Photograph home before downsizing begins.
- Photograph each room and the finer details.
- Photograph large furnishings individually.
- Photograph key dinnerware pieces.

- Photograph treasured clothing items individually.
- Photograph sentimental home decor items individually.

Collections:

- Photograph prized collections as a whole.
- Photograph collection items individually.
- Photograph individual keepsakes.
- Reduce prized collections to 5-10 favorite pieces.
- Give away collections that will be gold to someone else: Family Members, Garage / Estate Sales, Find collectors or museums, Charity collection centers.
- Trash the rest.

Documents:

- Give away binders and files you no longer wish to maintain to family members interested in the work.
- Give away binders and files you no longer wish to maintain to researchers actively working on the line that you discover through connections on genealogy websites.
- Give away binders and files for family lines you no longer wish to maintain to genealogy libraries or historical societies.
- Process the piles, files, and binders, for any family line you are actively researching.
- Trash all papers that are photocopies and family group sheets with no identified sources.
- Remove images and place images in the photo piles.
- Process family group sheets that have sources on them by adding information to digitized tree. Trash the charts when finished.
- Process copies of documents by comparing them to online sources. If they are online, discard the papers. If they are not, keep digitize the documents then trash the photo copies.
- Keep original or near-original genealogical documents.

- Reduce the organization of the papers to the fewest files or binders as possible.

- Trash all other papers based on Downsizing Quick Guides (link can be found in the *Action Plans* chapter at the end of this book).

Photos:

- Trash blurry, duplicate, or inappropriate photos.

- Trash photos with an unclear or confusing purpose.

- Keep photos that are labeled.

- Process photos that are not labeled by asking family members what they know, organizing photos to see if you can determine who the individual was, or posting in online forums.

- Give away unidentified photos to archives, libraries, or genealogical societies (if applicable).

- Post images on websites like Dead Fred to find possible leads.

- Trash all photos and photo albums with unidentified individuals that you were unable to determine in 12 months.

Media:

- Process slides and negatives by sifting through the images and keeping only the ones that depict people and buildings.

- Trash the remaining slides and negatives.

- Digitize slides and negatives by outsourcing the project.

- Trash the slides and negative after they are digitized. (You could keep them in archival boxes of reduced size only if you have space to maintain the photos in your new space.)

- Photograph book, magazine, movie, and music collections as a whole.

- Photograph individual historically significant items.

- Keep genealogy methodology and resource books that you are actively using.

- Keep story-based family history books and home movies.
- Find a collector or museum for historical media.
- Trash books, magazines, movies, music.
- Trash chart based family histories.
- Trash outdated genealogy methodology and resource books.
- Digitize home movies, audio recording, performances of relatives.
- Trash the decaying media after digitization is complete.

6 Months Before Downsize Deadline

Furnishing, Housewares, Clothing, Lifestyle Items:

- Give away any previously determined or specified inheritance items to heirs.
- Keep furnishings, clothing, and lifestyle items essential items you will move to use in the new space.
- Keep furnishings, clothing, and lifestyle items that fit in the new space and have sentimental value.
- Give away furnishings, clothing, personal effects that will be gold to someone else: Family Members, Museums or Collectors, Garage / Estate Sales, Online selling sites, Charity collection centers.
- Trash large furnishings, clothing, personal effects, and home decor from the home that are broken, do not sell, or are unacceptable to charity collection centers.

What is the biggest difference between the 3-5 month plan and the 12 month plan?

When you have 12 months or more to downsize, you can contact archives, libraries, societies, and museums about donating anything in your home to them. They are not a charitable donation dumping ground. These institutions have small staffs and need to know what is coming before they accept it.

You will need time to find these repositories that want your items and follow their instructions for donations. You might have to organize your collection. You might have to provide evidence of the person who owned the item and their connection to the local area.

In short, donating to archives, libraries, societies, and museums takes a considerable amount of time. If you have 12 months or more to downsize, you can explore these options. Otherwise, you will be better off foregoing this path.

Additionally, with 12 months, you can spend more time digitizing before and during your downsizing process. As such, you will be able to preserve more and have less guilt when a sizable amount of your possessions are reduced by 50% or more.

Finally, with 12 months, you can photograph more of your possessions individually rather than as a collection. You can also photograph the smallest of details. Granted, you will have image overwhelm on your hard drive, but that might be a better problem to have should you want to recall a memory.

Assess Your Household

Once you know what your action plan is, you will do well to assess the scope of what you have to downsize. Be advised, if you have 1 hour to grab what you can, you will skip this step entirely. If you have a weekend, your assessment will be bare bones. Identify the rooms and call it good.

If you have inherited a few boxes, your assessment will be completed in a matter of seconds. If you have a 3,000 square foot home with a attic, a garage, a storage shed, and an off-site storage unit, you will have an assessment that will take a couple of hours to create.

The longer your timeline, the more detailed your assessment can be. Be careful to not waste time you could be spending downsizing by being too detailed. You just want an overview so you can allocate time and break up the project into manageable parts.

Why create an assessment?

An assessment reduces the need to pull everything out of a home, attic, or box, and pile it up in one heap on the front lawn that probably will tempt you to light a match and start a bonfire or attract garage sale hunters looking for bargains.

Basic Assessment

For those with homes and storage spaces, your assessment will begin by identifying the rooms in your home's and the other storage units you have to process.

Your assessment may include:

Master Bedroom	Play Room
Guest Bedroom	Attic
Spare Bedroom	Basement
Additional Bedroom(s)	Cellar
Master Bathroom	Garage
Guest Bathroom	Patio
Additional Bathroom(s)	Porch
Living Room	Staircase
Dining room	Sun room
Kitchen	TV room
Pantry	Workshop
Breakfast Room	Shed
Den / Study	Storage Units
Office	Utility Room
Hallway	Breezeway
Laundry Room	

It is possible this list is overlooking a room or storage space that is specific to your needs. Add to this list.

Expanded Assessment

If you have 3 months or more to downsize your home, you can expand the basic assessment to include the more specific spaces in your home or storage units. Detail the number of rooms, closets, bookcases, dressers, drawers, wall shelves, cabinets, and cubbies within each room or space listed on the Basic Assessment. See the following example.

Master Bedroom :

dressers ___

side tables ___

closets

desks

bookcases

cedar chests

List wall decorations:

pictures

art

shelf displays

List collections:

dolls

hats

jewelry

art work

Office :

desks ___

side tables ___

closets

filing cabinets

built in shelves

wall shelves

bookcases

List items on the floor:

plants

lamps

rugs

furniture

List collections:

books

awards

decorative glasses

Implement the Plan

Once you have selected the Action Plan that reflects your time constraints and inventoried the project you have to downsize, you can make a plan that will achieve your downsizing goals and preserve the most valuable family history along the way. Plans should contain enough detail to explain to others who may be helping you without them constantly asking for assistance. Tasks should be small enough (1-2 hours) so that helpers can complete them during the time they are volunteering. By having a list of small tasks that are checked off when completed, you can start to see how much of your project you have accomplished.

Downsizing – Step by Step

1. Determine which rooms should be processed first.
2. Put dates (or times) next to rooms that need to be processed.
3. Determine who, if not yourself, will process that room.
4. Prepare to downsize with boxes and containers that can help with the sorting process labeled: Keep, Give away, Process, Trash, Strays

How to Handle Strays

Have you ever spring cleaned your home and discovered how many things migrated throughout your house away from their intended storage space? It happens to us all the time. We find game pieces in piano books, hearing aides in clothes closets, and toy cars in kitchen cabinets. Sometimes "strays" are a collection spread through several rooms of a house. When strays are not with the like items, downsizing decisions become difficult.

While processing a room, have an extra box for strays. No one should leave a room to corral the strays. Return strays to the appropriate room after sorting a room, box, or closet. Remind yourself, and any assistants, to not make final determinations about reducing a room until they check the stray boxes before any irreversible decisions are made.

After stray items return to their correct location, you could further process your possessions. A game may suddenly become something that can be sold at a garage sale because it now has all of its pieces. You may also have to reevaluate the 3-5 items you saved from a collection because the stray item has more value than the others.

How to Downsize With Others

Working with others to downsize your home, or that of a loved one may be a blessing or a curse. These tips may simplify the working relationship.

1. Use tags if working with others
2. Tag items that will be relocated to your new space.
3. Tag items that will go to heirs or family members.
4. Tag items that should be photographed before they are given away or trashed.

If you have people helping you pare down the possessions in a home during a weekend, assign them a room or storage space. Give them the appropriate Downsizing Quick Guides (link can be found in the *Action Plans* chapter at the end of this book) and five boxes (listed above). If they have questions about an item, have them set it aside in the process pile or box. Consult the Basic Assessment Plan to keep everyone on track.

If you have a 3 month or longer time frame and someone offers to help, the Expanded Assessment will reduce the size of the tasks they will handle. They can process one closet, one bookcase, one file cabinet, or one dresser. An assistant will likely be more helpful with a smaller set of decisions to make but they will still need to refer to the Downsizing Quick Guides (link can be found in the *Action Plans* chapter at the end of this book).

PRESERVE: Digitize Your Family History

While downsizing your home or inheritance, you should photograph the household and its collections before you decrease them. You should sift through your photos, documents, videos, and audio recordings. Now you need to focus on digitizing the remaining media for preservation and sharing.

Photograph an Overview of Everything

Before you downsizing your possessions, preserve the home at that moment in time with your camera. Practice the film maker's art of zooming from wide to narrow, so you capture perspective as well as individual details.

Begin by photographing the exterior of the living space including porches, gardens, workshops, garages, sheds, orchards, the backyard, and more. Focus on individual yard decorations as time permits if you know the story behind each item.

Then photograph the interior of the home. Photograph each room as a whole. If time permits, shoot each room using different angles (looking down in, looking up from the floor) and entrances. The living spaces will never return to this arrangement again, so capture your or your loved one's living space.

Now focus your attention on photographing the collections including wall art, framed portraits, housewares, movies, books, games, music, souvenirs, keepsakes, clothing, antiques, awards, ties, jewelry, and collectibles. Zoom in on individual items within a collection as time permits.

When you have photographed the home and belongings, you can begin reducing your belongings.

Tips for Digitizing Your Photos, Documents, and Media During the Initial Downsize

If you have a 3-12 month timeline to downsize, skip to tips on how to digitize specific media included in this chapter.

If you have a shorter timeline to decrease your possessions, have two boxes between your Keep and Process piles. Label the first box Outsourcing and the second DIY. As you sift through your belongings:

- Place all videos, audio records, slides, and negatives in the outsourcing box.
- Place all photos and original and near-original documents in the DIY box.
- Leave all process documents in the process file.

When you have finished the initial reduction of your possessions, fine-tune the saved photos, documents, and media using the principles taught in the chapter *REDUCE: Evaluate Your Photos and Media*.

Upon completing the fine-tuned decrease of photos and media, send items in the Outsourcing box to a digitization service. Meanwhile, begin digitizing items in the DIY box. Tackle the things in the process box after you empty your Outsource and DIY boxes.

Photography Basics

If you are a talented photographer, skip this section. If you define your photography skills as novice or amateur, follow these tips to capture the best image you can of your family treasures no matter the camera you have.

Use a tripod whenever possible.

Amazon sells tripods for digital cameras, smartphones, and tablets. USE THEM! Since your home and possessions do not move, you may drastically increase the clarity of your images by mounting your camera on a tripod.

Ensure that the tripod you purchase has a full range of tilting options. The tripod should have the ability to orient your camera in a horizontal or vertical position, focus straight ahead or aim nearly directly below. The more range of motion your tripod mount has, the easier your task of photographing your possessions becomes.

Opt for a full-sized tripod rather than the mini-mounts. Full-sized tripods allow you the widest range of options for photographing your objects.

You can photograph your home and possessions without a tripod if your camera has a high-quality anti-shake setting. However, when shooting small items, you can not beat the quality of the images taken with tripod-mounted cameras.

Use enough light.

In an ideal world, you would photograph your possessions when you have natural light that casts soft and poorly defined shadows rather than harsh, clearly defined shadows as if you stood outside at noon on a sunny day. When the ideal is not available, you can use filtered light using a softbox cover to a light source or place small objects in a lightbox.

Numerous blogs and YouTube videos have instructions on creating and using do-it-yourself lightboxes and softbox covers. You could purchase a lightbox, such as Shotbox, that will have the perfect light every time. The camera mount for the Shotbox is an added bonus.

When photographing an object, have enough light that you can see the finer details of the object or room. Avoid too much light that reflects back off the items you are photographing. However, you have to do the very best you can with what you have.

Keep your background simple

As you begin to photograph collections and individual items, move them away from their regular location. For small and medium-sized objects, shoot them in a lightbox. Opt for a white or black solid-colored backdrop. White and light colored items generally look best on black. Dark and bright colored pieces look best on white.

For larger pieces, like clothing and furniture, find a location where the floor and wall are the same color. Thus, your eye is not drawn to the floor-wall color change rather than the object. If you lack such a location, tack a wrinkle-resistant fabric to a wall and then let flow onto a floor. Soften the hard angle created where the floor meets the wall by pulling the fabric away from that junction. If you need to visualize this set up better, search for blog posts and YouTube videos for DIY seamless backdrops.

By simplifying the backdrop behind your objects, you can emulate near magazine quality image.

Photograph the small details

The final basic tip for photographing your treasures involves zooming in and focusing on the fine details of an object. You can plop a doll, a fork, a vase, or a watch on your solid background and snap a photo and call it good. However, if you will pay attention to the smallest details, you will capture a memory.

Zoom in on the engravings on the side of a ring. Photograph the backside of bracelets to see the personal inscriptions. Focus in on the stitching of a nine-block from a larger quilt.

The list of small details is endless because of the variety of objects you can photograph. Photograph a piece as a whole, and then zoom in for a closer inspection.

Additionally, pay attention to the small details and their arrangement in your photograph. Arrange a wristwatch so that the 12 o'clock position is to the left or the top of your image rather than the right. When you photograph several objects in a group, arrange them, so they are facing toward each other or in the same direction, depending on the story you wish to convey.

You can research more tips on photographing small objects, but the above four tips will quickly enhance your pictures with ease.

Cameras generally capture the three-dimensional objects around your home. You might have to use a camera to photograph pictures that you can not remove from frames without damaging the image. A camera may also digitally capture Family

Bibles without damaging the fragile binding. You can even turn your camera into a scanner for your photos and documents. However, scanners generally do a better job of creating a high-quality image of your pictures and documents in the most efficient manner.

Preserve Your Documents and Photos Through Scanning

If a document or photo lays flat and is smaller than 8 ½ by 11, use a scanner to digitize it. Scanning can efficiently digitize loose pictures or those removed from envelopes, frames, or albums. Scanners work well on original or near-original genealogical documents.

You can also scan some over-sized, flat items in sections. You will first scan overlapping portions of the photo or document. Using photo editing software such a Photoshop, you can digitally stitch the separate sections together. Mobile scanners can also photograph and stitch together images of over-sized items. Follow the instructions in the user's manual to accomplish this task.

Organize before you begin.

Scan only the gold and process piles of photos and documents for the family lines you decided to curate. If you are processing a stack of research that you will donate elsewhere, scan only the original and near original documents.

When you downsize your photo collection, we recommend you chronologically organize the pictures. Retain this chronological arrangement, though you may wish to divide the photos by surnames or families. In so doing, you will create a visual timeline of a person's or family's life. You will also have similarly colored photographs grouped together, which makes scanning much more efficient. Scanners with similarly colored pictures can evenly and more accurately apply color-corrective technology to your images.

Now, organize your documents by surname and then by document type. Perhaps you plan to maintain original records and photos for your Smith and Townsend lines. You will separate all records about your Smith line from your Townsend line. Then place all of the pension records, death certificates, bible records, and so forth for the Smith line into separate piles, and repeat the process for your Townsend line. Organizing your physical documents will speed up the digital organization process and keep the research for specific families together.

Consider Outsourcing the Scanning

A scan may take up to 3 minutes to process each time you tell the computer to make a digital image. A collection of 2,000 photos or documents can easily take 100 hours when scanned individually at the highest resolution. Consider whether you want to outsource the scanning or do it yourself.

Outsourcing saves you precious time you can use for other downsizing tasks. Digitization companies can process 10-gallon bins of photos in a matter of hours. You will likely take a month or longer. Additionally, the scanning company will also crop your images, so you will not necessarily need to learn photo editing software to separate your pictures. If you hire a company to digitize your photos and paper files, make sure you only send gold, and not chrome plastic, so you economize the process.

If you scan photos yourself, make sure you have eliminated blurry images, duplicates and unidentified persons from your collection, as mentioned in the chapter *REDUCE: Evaluate Your Photos and Media*. Do not waste all of your precious time preserving chrome plastic.

Learn how to scan in batches. Scan as many pictures as you can fit on the scanner bed without the images touching. Ensure they have the same color processing - black and white with black and white, sepia with sepia, color with color. You can go a step further and group the faded red colored images from 1970s separate from the flash photography images of the 1990s. By working with batches, you will spend less time scanning and more time separating images in a photo editing program. Leaving space between the pictures enables some programs to separate the scanned images at the click of a button.

Scanning your photos yourself may save you money so you can reserve funds for digitizing other media. You must have a long timeline to process the images and the computer skills necessary to accomplish the task.

Realistically evaluate your scanning project. If you have 2,000+ images to scan, you should definitely consider outsourcing the project. If your document and image collection is much smaller, then you should attempt to tackle it yourself.

Which scanner should you use?

Although scanners come in a variety of options, the most common scanners are flatbeds. Most new home scanners produce similar quality images. As such, you will not need a top of the line scanner to convert your family history files to a digital format, no matter what your tech-loving relatives may tell you.

Avoid using document feed scanners for fragile photos, photos attached to other pages, or pages with plastic film on top. The resulting images are poor quality, and the feed scanner will often jam and likely damage your photos or documents.

Avoid wand scanners. Wand scanners often distort the images if you misuse it.

If you do not have access to a flatbed scanner, you can use mobile technology. You could purchase a portable scanner and produce high-quality images. Your tablet and smartphone may also accomplish the scanning task utilizing a variety of apps. Use what you have readily available and know how to operate.

If you need to learn to scan, realize that the skill improves with practice. If your first hour of scanning produces three digitized images, you will likely decrease the time necessary to process 1,000 photos with enough practice. Thus, do not pick an option that takes 10 minutes to learn and produces poor quality scans. Pick the option that provides high-quality images but has the shallowest learning curve for you.

Use a high DPI.

Scan your photos at a minimum of 300 dpi. For small images, such as a 2 in x 2 in or smaller, scan them at 600 or 1200 dpi. This allows you to use the image in at a larger size in other projects. If you have photos that need touch-up or restoration work, scan the picture at 1200 dpi.

Many genealogists prefer all photos saved as TIF files. TIF files take up a lot of storage space. If you have infinite storage space, then save your images as TIFs. If you lack sufficient storage space, save most of your pictures as JPG. If you plan on restoring a photo, then TIF is best.

Store the Gold

When you have finished scanning your photos and documents, store the gold. Find archival quality containers for your photos. Save only the original and near original documents in files. Your pictures and historical document collections should have decreased significantly.

Digitize Your Genealogy Research

With your photos and historical documents digitized, you can now focus on digitizing your genealogy research notes and charts from your Keep and Process piles. You will also compare your photocopies of records, such as census records, vital records, and other easily accessible documents online.

Digitize With Genealogy Programs

As you previously sorted your piles, files, books, and binders, you may have a lot of research papers. If you have not converted to paperless genealogy research, you need to do this now. There are no ifs, ands, or buts about it. If you want your family to have access to your years of research, you need to embrace technology and transfer your notes, trees, and charts into a genealogy software program at the very least and in online trees at best.

If you have been a conscientious researcher with notebooks, research reports, and research logs, you will want to opt for a genealogy database that will meet your needs. These programs cater to advanced researchers and have forms to corral your To-Do lists, research reports, timelines, narratives, notes, conclusions, correspondence, pedigree charts, family group sheets, research logs, and more.

You will record citations for your original and near original documents in the source fields of your programs. You will also add source citations for the photocopies of records, such as census records, vital records, and more.

Depending on your genealogy program, you can then share your research on FamilySearch, Ancestry, or other websites. In so doing, you will investigate whether these platforms have easy to access version of the photocopied documents you have retained. As you discover census records, vital records, city directories, and additional records on FamilySearch, Ancestry, and the like, you can discard the physical print out of those records.

Will your database last long into the future?

Genealogy databases are primarily tools for research projects. They can organize and maintain your research logs, notes, and correspondence. It will be up to your posterity to update your database to the latest version, so as not to lose your work. As such, you will want to ensure a genealogist in the family receives a copy of your database.

You may also upload a GEDCOM version of your research to FamilySearch under their genealogy section. This file will not absorb into the collaborate family tree but rather remain as is for researchers to consult through the genealogy section of the website.

Digitize With Online Trees

Online trees reduce the need for your descendants to upgrade to the latest genealogy program to access their family history research. To preserve your family history for the maximum number of family members, upload your information to an online tree.

Take into consideration that some websites require your relatives to pay a fee to access their family history. Some online trees can provide free access to your accounts. Do not choose an online platform entirely based on the cost of access to your research. Not every website will exist in the future. FamilySearch has the backing of the Family History Library in Salt Lake City. As such, the site and its supporting agencies have preserved family histories since the late 1800s. Incorporate the FamilySearch website in your preservation plans.

While adding your genealogical research to online trees, you will likely discover that much of your information already appears online in multiple tree websites. As you come across the previously digitized tree, you can add new information and speed up your digitization process.

If you are a casual hobbyist or inherited someone else's genealogical papers, use a free collaborative online tree. Your current options include FamilySearch (free), WikiTree (free), or Geni (free). At the time of printing this book, FamilySearch has the largest database, but WikiTree and Geni attract more serious researchers. If you opt to use a paid online tree, such as Ancestry, then only upload your genealogy gold. Leave your genealogy chrome plastic on other websites.

Collaborative trees allow you to compare your genealogical research to the content already accessible online without you having to build a tree from scratch. You may discover that your research already appears in these trees and you do not need to take further action. When a tree lacks the information you have gathered, you will update the profiles on the trees and record where you obtain your information. After you compare all of your paper files to the online trees, you will discard your chrome plastic documents and store the gold.

Additionally, you will compare the photocopies of the records you have kept. If the paper has a document that is not easily accessible online, then save the physical copy in your gold pile. If the source, such as a census record, military draft record, or passenger list, is available online, then create a link to a person's profile of the digitized source. Some websites, such as FamilySearch and

Ancestry, may simplify the process by providing hints to such documents.

As you upload your tree to an online website, you may consider uploading to Ancestry, MyHeritage or other sites. You will have the option to mark your tree as private. Private online trees may keep your research from being stolen, but if you pass away without passing on access to your private tree, no one benefits. You will need to provide access to your accounts in your will if you choose the private tree option. Public trees require no such designation and can, therefore, live on long after you leave this world.

What about the research you no longer wish to curate?

For research that you no longer wish to curate and cannot find someone willing to receive your research, then add the information to FamilySearch, WikiTree, or Geni. If you want to add the information to all three websites quickly, then:

1. Add the information to FamilySearch
2. Download it to the program called RootsMagic
3. Save a GEDCOM file from RootsMagic to your computer.
4. Upload the GEDCOM files to WikiTree and Geni

If you have the time and desire to process this research, you will transform your chrome plastic into someone else's genealogy gold.

Cautions About Updating Collaborative Trees

In collaborative online trees, do not change a name, date, place, or relationship if your paper tree lacks supporting documentation for your desired changes. Perhaps you have a paper identifying Johnny as a child of Bob. Unfortunately, it does not indicate who provided the information. When you view Bob's profile on an online collaborative tree, you notice that Johnny does not appear as Bob's child. Do not add Johnny to Bob's family based on an unsourced paper. Instead, create a note mentioning the possibility of Bob having a son named Johnny, as discovered in your files.

Then ask if anybody can substantiate this fact. By leaving a note, you are preserving the possibility for others to investigate.

Digitize Family History Books and Journals

If published family histories, unpublished manuscripts, and journals appear in your Keep or Process boxes, you may not know how to treat them. Should you scan them? If so, how? Is there anything else you should consider to preserve these items better?

Depending on the age of the family history, county history, city directory, yearbook or biography, you might discover a copy of the book at a library, archive or online. Visit WorldCat and online library and archive catalog pages. Some books appear online on websites such as FamilySearch, Ancestry, Google Books, HathiTrust, and the Internet Archive (to name a few available at the time of this printing). Enter in the title of your book to determine whether a copy appears on a library or archive shelf somewhere in the world.

If multiple copies exist, you can discard the yearbooks, city directories and county directories. If you have a published family history, you can keep it if you have space or give it away to family members.

If you have an unpublished family history, with charts representing more than 75% of the content, you should have trashed this already. However, if you kept the family history for the 25% which represents stories, then extract the stories by typing in the content into a word processing program or using an OCR scanner. Cite the original source for the material. If you wrote a story-focused family history, then make plans to finish the book. Read the chapter *SHOWCASE: Display What You Love* for tips on publishing books.

Finally, if you do not find a published book of genealogical significance online, scan the book to ensure you do not have the only copy of the book in case it is destroyed by a flood (this actually happened to me). Once the book is digitized, search for an archive, library, or genealogy society that would welcome the physical copy of the book. You may discover entities that will accept the digitized version of the book, but you will have to research the requirements about copyright restrictions.

When you have handwritten journals, scan or photograph them. If the binding is fragile, you will need to use a camera. After digitizing the journal, share the images with family members or volunteers who will volunteer to transcribe these handwritten pieces.

The ability to read the handwriting of the past becomes more difficult as each generation passes. Think of the scripts from the 1700s. That handwriting differs significantly from scripts used between the 1800s and 1900s. Take time to transcribe the written items so future generations can read them.

You can key it in yourself or use a voice-to-text service such as Dragon Dictation or the Voice Typing feature in Google Docs. You might also want to transcribe the journals by reading them aloud while your smartphone, tablet, or computer records your voice. Then use a paid online transcription service to convert your spoken words into typed text quickly. Some transcription services are as inexpensive as $0.10 a minute.

Depending on the service, you may receive a better transcription if you pay for human review of the transcription. For auto transcriptions, you will need to edit the text to correct any transcription errors but correcting the mistakes is faster than typing the entire journal.

Once you have transcribed the journal, you may find a repository willing to add the physical book and the transcription to their collection. You may find family members who wish to maintain the journal. The transcription and digital images of the journal can appear in family history projects discussed in the chapter SHOW-CASE: Display What You Love.

Digitize Slides, Negatives, and Audio/Visual Media

Most people should outsource the digitization of slides, negatives, and audio/visual material. These companies have the time, skills, or the equipment necessary to digitize your difficult media.

When contracting with a professional company, research their capabilities. Make sure they can handle any problem, which include moldy videos, broke cassette tapes, and over-sized photos. Ask whether they will charge you for blank negatives or film footage. Find out how materials will be returned to you physically and in digital formats.

Recognize that cheaper is not always better. Costco can handle some projects, but not many. A former photo lab that focuses on preservation might be better, especially if they are local. If you do not have a quality local option, many companies around the United States offer this service.

Slides & Negatives

There are several DIY tutorials online on how to convert slides and negatives. There are also negative and slide scanners that you can purchase for home use. In our experience, converting slides and negatives at home is tedious and often produces a low-quality image.

Before you digitize these materials, determine if a decent quality print exists. You can save money scanning a good quality print than digitizing a slide or negative.

Although you can digitize these items yourself, you will often have better results and less hassle by sending slides and negatives to a digitizing company. Follow the advice in the chapter REDUCE: Evaluate Your Photos and Media to ensure you only develop likely family history gold rather than chrome plastic.

Audio & Video Media

Converting audio and video reels to digital formats stabilize the memories and make them suitable for easy viewing. The sooner you digitize these items, the better the image quality appears.

Few people can play reel to reel films, audio cassette tapes, and VHS films. Therefore, you should hire digital duplication service providers to digitize your audio/visual media. Keep in mind that the companies you hire have to follow copyright laws, so the tapes you wish converted should be family history in nature. Again, what you have at this stage should have been reduced during the downsizing phase to your genealogy gold or some items that have golden moments.

Search locally and online for services that can convert your cassettes to MP3s. You will want companies that can convert videos to MP4s and other digital formats. Shop around for service providers in your area or that allow you to ship your media through the mail with a tracking code throughout the entire process.

Digitization Leads To More Downsizing

After reducing your possessions and digitizing your family history gold and useful chrome plastic, you have succeeded where most others fail.

This phase started with four categories:

1. Keep
2. Process
3. Give Away
4. Trash (although you should empty the trash bin often)

You also may have the following temporary boxes:

1. Strays
2. Outsource Digitization
3. DIY Digitization

The Stray box disappeared at the end of your downsizing process as you returned items to their proper location for final decision making. The digitization boxes should empty as you accomplish the tasks in this chapter. Once digitized, items will migrate to the Keep, Give Away or Trash boxes.

You now have to tackle the tough decisions in your Processing box. Ultimately, your Process box will no longer exist.

You may have saved items you could not part during your initial downsizing. After photographing or scanning these items, you should recognize whether the object or paper is gold or chrome plastic disguised as gold. You must now discard the chrome plastic if you have not already.

You might not want to part with your master's thesis or old letters. During the sorting process, you should have discarded classroom notes which led up to your master's degree. You should also have disposed of letters lacking family history significance. Now, you will digitize these papers. You will likely then discard the thesis but find room for the correspondence in your new space.

You may have saved boxes of childhood mementos because of your short timeline. The desire to share these treasures with your children is noble. But as the years pass, if you never pulled out the box to showcase the keepsakes, you have clutter. While you downsized, you may have known the box contained chrome plastic but could still not set it aside. After you photograph the objects, you will need to keep very few of them. Downsize your treasures further. Then turn your attention to writing stories about the keepsakes and adding the photo and story to family history projects, which you will read about in the chapter *SHOWCASE: Display What You Love.*

In the end, you gain more by having less. You will not lose your memories by converting them from physical items to digital files. You will preserve your family heritage. After you digitize the physical media, you will discover you can discard many photos, documents, videos, and audio recordings and gain even more space in your new home.

You now need to turn your attention to properly organizing and storing your items in the Keep box, finding new homes for the Give Away box, and then emptying out the Trash one final time.

PRESERVE: Labeling and Storing

After digitizing your downsized possessions, you should no longer have a Process box. In this chapter, you will focus on preserving family history items in your Keep box and digital files on your computer.

Label What You Keep

If you keep physical copies of photos, documents, and artifacts of family history value, you must label them if you want them to remain valuable. Essentially, these items should not have stayed in your possession this far if you could not identify them. The labeling phase of downsizing with family history in mind ensures those who care for your belongings after you can identify the value as well.

If you have photos that lack identifying information, but you know it, you must record it now. If you have original or near-original genealogically significant documents, you must label the folders in which they are contained. For artifacts that you will not showcase in your home, you must clearly mark the archival quality boxes in which they are preserved.

Whatever you fail to label will inadvertently wind up in the garbage even though you downsized intending to prevent such actions.

Ensure that every photo you keep from this point forward clearly identifies the subject of the picture. Ensure that every document you keep clearly denotes who is the subject of the paper. For every keepsake, you save, record to whom it belonged and the story behind it.

How to label photos

When you label photos, use an archival pen or pencil. We prefer pens as pencils tend to fade. Write on the back of photos which you place on a clean work surface. Write lightly but clearly. Set aside the pictures until the ink dries so it does not transfer to other photos.

Some archivists suggest you do not write on photos or documents. Instead, you should store the pictures and documents in polypropylene sleeves and including a piece of acid-free paper and record the information on the separate paper. Others suggest writing information on labels that you stick to the polypropylene sleeves. You do not know who will receive your photo collection after you have it. You can not predict how people will handle your photo and document collection after you. Therefore, we suggest you keep the picture and identifying information permanently together by writing on the back of the photo or document whenever possible.

What to Write on Photos

Identify the who, what, when, where, and how of the photos.

Use full dates and names as much as possible. "Uncle Bubba in 16 at Schuller" is not helpful.

Is Uncle Bubba actually Bob, Raymond, or Johan?

Is the year 1916 or is he age 16?

Is that Schuller's home, park, city, or county?

Researchers may accurately guess based on the quality of the film, but they should not need to if you do your part. Provide a first and last name whenever possible, and a middle if you have repetitions names in your family such as my family full of Robert Zumsteins.

Strive for a full date, such as 16 November 1936. If all you can determine is Easter 1934, that will suffice. If you only know, the summer of 1866, that works too.

When you identify places, include something beyond a nickname. Add Schuller Park in Columbus, Ohio to clearly identify a location.

Keep the Labeling System Simple

When you label your archive boxes, ensure your identification system does not require an advanced degree in asset management to understand. Record on the outside, what the box contains and the surname, or individual, to which it belonged.

Whenever possible, insert an archival quality paper that provides further details about the items inside. For the Family Bible, record the original owner of the scriptures and who the custodians of the book have been over time. For clothing, textiles, or other artifacts, insert a biographical sketch about the original owner and any story you have about the object. Give the gift of meaning to your preserved treasures by saving the who, what, when, where and why behind the objects alongside the actual item.

Building Your Family Archive

While you processed your family archive in preparation for downsizing and digitizing, you should have used the cheapest and most disposable containers until you could finish these two tasks. You should not dispose of archival quality containers during the downsizing and digitizing phase and thereby negatively affect what has been preserved thus far. If you did not have your family treasures in archival-safe boxes, you will tackle that step now.

As you build your archive, strive to purchase the highest quality preservation materials, based on the constraints of space and finances for the items you have. Your family archive will not necessarily meet the same guidelines as another person. Do the best you can with what you have. If you can not achieve your ideal archive, consider finding an alternative home for your treasures, such as extended family members or museums, repositories, and libraries.

Storing Photos

When you store photos, you will either store them in albums or in boxes. What you choose depends on your collection and what space you have available.

Do not store "magnetic" photo albums. The photo albums seem magnetic because they utilized glue strips or dots on the acid paper pages that attracted photos like a magnet. These albums make removing photos difficult, and the glue ruins your pictures over time. Carefully slide a piece of dental floss between the image and the magnetic photo album page for any prints that are difficult to remove.

You can recreate the arrangement in a new, archival quality album which utilizes acid-free sleeves, sheet protectors, or photo corners. Another option is you can condense the photo collection to a chronologically organized photo box. Many archivists will balk at this suggestion, so take a picture of each album page before condensing your collection just in case the picture arrangement has genealogical clues.

For other albums, you can preserve them in archival-safe boxes. Insert archival grade tissue between each page to help protect the individual pages. If the album is in fair condition with the binding intact, you can store it in an upright box on a shelf. If the photo album is fragile, you will want a container that lays flat. Opt for a box that has an at least an inch of space around the photo album and then use acid-free tissue paper to prevent the book from moving inside the box.

For loose photos or photos you removed from albums, you have various levels of archival suggestions. One archivist suggests storing each photo individually in archival sleeves and then placing those images in a water-resistant plastic box, laid flat from the bottom of the box to the top. Others suggest archival quality boxes that look like shoe boxes but have better quality material. You will fill these boxes, not too much so that the photos bend from over stuffing, or not enough so that your pictures do not stand up straight.

What you use depends on the size of your photo collection and your pocketbook. Purchase the best quality solution given the constraints you have on space and finances.

Storing Documents

Spend time and money preserving only the documents for the surnames you desire to continue serving as curator. Your collection should only include original and near-original documents.

Remove any paper clips, rubber bands, and staples from your old documents. These items cause rapid deterioration of materials. Use the highest quality storage for your originals, such as archival grade polyethylene bags. Place each document in a separate bag and then file these documents in a binder designed for archival storage or in an archival-safe document storage box.

If you happen to still have chrome plastic documents in your collection, do not spend money placing them in an archival quality box. Use cheap, temporary folders for the chrome plastic for your research. Then give these items away when you have finished processing them.

Storing Family History Treasures

Use the best archival quality containers you can afford for your historically significant items. These items could be a family bible, a journal, or ceremonial clothing.

A wide variety of acid-free and lignin-free storage boxes are available that can accommodate your family history gold. A search for 'archival storage boxes' on Google or Amazon will return a long list of suppliers and options. Read reviews of suppliers and options before you make a final purchase.

You albums might fit best in storage boxes that have flat bottoms with hinged lids or a drop front. If you have fragile printed material, you might find envelope style containers to wrap the books. Portfolio cases and binder albums may work for your documents or photo collections. More boxes and containers abound for the various types of artifacts you have.

Each container style serves different purposes so take time to investigate which is the best option for your treasures. Archival storage boxes are worth the investment; however, keep the number of storage boxes you need to a minimum.

If you can not find a box that snuggly fits your artifact so it will not jostle inside, purchase a slightly larger container and then use crumpled archival tissue to keep the object from shifting around in the box.

If you have family bibles or rare books, you can place them in archival-safe polyethylene bags to prevent dust from accumulating on the items. These bags can also serve as a barrier in case water invades your home and attacks your archive. Then place these books inside an archival box.

Storing Your Archive

The ideal family archive stores your treasures off the floor, in a cool environmental away from vents, outside walls, and moisture fluctuations. You might not have that space available or in existence in your living space. Store your treasures as close to ideal as possible. Above all, do not store your family archive in attics, garages, or storage units

Instead, store your archival boxes in your living spaces. Consider ordering storage containers in one color and turn the boxes into a design element in your TV unit, or computer credenza.

Prioritize Your Archive

For most people, the expense of storing your treasures to the highest degree of archival quality exceeds their available funds. Therefore, you will spend more on storage for the irreplaceable items, such as the Family Bible, and less on trinkets, such as my pageant crown or souvenir collection.

Condense Your Archive

Although you want the highest quality boxes for your documents, consider the portability of your files should a disaster strike. Can you easily and quickly move your paper archive? If not, you need smaller containers or a small archive. Consider giving away more of your collection to meet a reasonable portability goal.

Also, consider who will eventually inherit your family archive. Is your archive small enough for the new custodian to handle? Will you have to break up the collection? If you do, who will receive each portion? Will they have the space to accommodate the family treasures?

You do not have to throw everything out and save nothing. Far from it. However, you may still need to downsize your treasures as you look to the future of your archive.

Protecting Your Digital Archive

With your family memories digitized, you must actively work to maintain your collection in the same way you would find a location for your physical archive that is temperature controlled and humidity free.

Save your digital data in multiple places. Your first option includes online trees, as mentioned in the chapter *PRESERVE: Digitize Your Family History*. Your online solution involves cloud services such as iDrive, Dropbox or GoogleDrive. You should also consider an automatic computer back up service such as Back-Blaze or Mozy.

External hard drives, DVDs, CDs, and thumb drives are slowly becoming obsolete. Use them for temporary back up services, but do not rely on them for long term solutions.

In addition to where you store your digital files, keep your data files updated. For now, MP3, MP4, and JPEG files are appropriate for your digital storage. However, if a new file type comes along in the future, you will want to update your digital files, so future generations have access to it.

Keep your genealogy software programs up-to-date. Several genealogy programs no longer exist. Some programs can not transfer all of your information to a new format because the GED-COM files do not preserve all the data. Ensure you are working with the latest version of your chosen genealogy program.

If you inherit a digital database program, hopefully there is a GEDCOM file that has been created using the outdated software.

GEDCOM is a file type very similar to TXT in that many applications can access the information, including online trees such as Ancestry.

Organize Your Digital Files

Follow the adage, "If you can not access it, your digital files are useless." The above advice focused on digital formats. These tips focus on digital file management.

Do Not Clutter Your Computer with Chrome Plastic

In previous chapters, you read how copies of census records, military records, and some vital records are chrome plastic. These records are easily accessible online, and you should not retain a physical copy of those images.

You should avoid cluttering your computer with these easy to access documents either. Utilize online trees, such as Family-Search, Ancestry, WikiTree, and Geni to manage links to the original images. If you do worry about the access to images changing, then only save files for research you are actively conducting and leave the rest online.

Organize Your Files By Type and By Family

When you organize your files on your computer, consider using a simple strategy. Keep images of people, places, and things separate from scans of documents.

Organize your pictures chronologically by family. You can separate a child from the family of his/her birth upon their marriage and the formation of a new family. All photos of them before this time remain in their parent's digital folder.

Alternately, File Your Documents by Surname and Then by Type

You can develop a more complex system than this, but for many people, this system is easy to understand and reduces the need for duplicate images. For more information about organizing your digital files, visit the Family History Fanatics YouTube Channel and find the video "How to Organize Digital Files for Genealogy Research."

Digitizing your possessions not only helps you reduce your household treasures but it is the format the future generations will relate to. With your belongings reduced and preserved, you can focus on reclaiming the space in your home and then showcasing your family history gold.

By digitizing the past, you ensure there will be personal history for your family in the future. They may not want the hard copies of heirlooms, collections, and research notes. They do want the memories of what matters most.

RECLAIM: Gain Space by Giving Away

As a little girl, I sang a song that had the line, "Love is something if you give it away, you will end up having more." When it comes to downsizing, your treasures become more valuable when you give some of them away. You will end up having more. Not more physical possessions but more of what you love around you. The things you part with will receive better homes and purposes.

You will primarily give away possessions by using them, giving them to family members, or giving them to non-family members.

Use It Up

Numerous families have never used particular articles of furniture, clothing, and dinnerware. Use these items today.

Andy and I both grew up with fine china that was rarely used for meals. Andy's parents allowed his family to use the dinnerware for special occasions. My parents only allowed dinner guests to use one set of china during dinner parties.

When both our parents downsized, they could not believe their children did not want the china they painstakingly moved from home to home. They attempted to sell the dinner sets only to discover no interested buyers. If only they had used the dinnerware to make memories while the kids grew up. The children, and now grandchildren, might have broken the china, but the memories would last forever.

You may have couches no one ever sat on, vases that never held flowers, and dresses no one ever wore. Use the sofa, pottery, clothing and more to make memories with your family now.

Survey after survey reveals how the Millennial and Gen Z cohorts do not wish to inherit this high-quality stuff. Those young adults are your heirs. Since they do not want your things, you might as well use your treasures. Finally, allow yourself to relax if a dress tears, a quilt becomes soiled, or a plate breaks. Focus on making memories or enjoying your possessions. If you cannot, give them away.

Give To Family, Now

Make the inheritance process easier by gifting your family your treasures now. Do not force heirs to wait until the reading of your will. Gifting items during your lifetime reduces estate hassles after you pass. Once you give something away, families cannot fight over who receives what.

Do not hold on to anything you can give away now to the intended recipient. If you have photo albums which a genealogy loving niece cannot wait to receive, send it to her now. If you have an antique rifle that your grandson admires, gift it to him now.

Perhaps you have not considered what items your heirs should receive. Start making those decisions. To assist in your decision-making process, make an inventory of your possessions. Ask your relatives what they would most wish to receive. You may discover your heirs want very little. If multiple relatives show interest in the same item, make your decision based on who will treasure it more.

If you have military regalia from grandpa, decide the best heir to receive these items. Is it the crazy pack rat aunt or the grand-child who served in the military? If you have an antique thimble collection or sewing machine, determine who will benefit from having such items. Is it the relative who loves sewing or the one who will stash the items in a garage?

While passing on your personal belongings, share the stories behind the items. The receiver will treasure your 'junk' more because they know the meaning behind them.

Realize some family members will use your belongings rather than painstakingly treasure them. Find joy in their actions. If you have a box of toys and old clothes, send them to young children or grandchildren who will enjoy playing with them. Gift belts, ties, dishes, books, games, dolls, and so on to family members who will put them to use.

Even though we suggest you gift items to your heirs now, do not feel obligated to have a barren home. If you enjoy having your dolls in a doll cabinet in your new home, then keep them. Just limit yourself to one doll cabinet and give away the china cabinet, two cedar chests, and a gun rack full of stuff. Pick one. Okay, pick two, but that is it!

For the items you do keep, list who will receive what in your will. Then have the document notarized. This should help courts facing feuding family members determine who should receive what according to your desires. (Mind you, we are not lawyers so do not quote us, but it would not hurt.)

Give To Non-Family

Opt to donate or sell your belongings to individuals outside of your family. We will list opportunities to do this in order of easiest to more difficult or time-consuming to accomplish. We cannot guarantee you will find a ready recipient for every item you wish to give away in the time you have available. As the number of baby boomers with vast estates of keepsakes that their families no longer want increasingly attempt to offload their household items, the fewer options you may have available.

Donation Centers

You will find charitable donation centers in many neighborhoods and communities. Finding one requires you to use a map or ask a neighbor where to find the closest center. To donate your belongings, drive up during business hours, and a volunteer will take your items from you.

There are some things they will not accept, such as old televisions, stuffed animals, photos and genealogical papers. They will accept many usable furnishings clothing, and lifestyle items.

Donation centers are the fastest way to dispose of your household items. Use them as much as possible when you have a short timeline to downsize.

Sell

You may attempt to sell your possessions through yard sales, estate sales, or online. Selling takes time, but you can organize an estate sale for a deceased loved one if you have a month to downsize.

If you have action figures, dolls, ceramics, comic books, and other collectibles, you could explore the possibility of selling your items online. If you have a month or longer to sell your belongings in this fashion, the cost to list an item that does not sell may be nominal.

Price your items to sell rather than to obtain the highest possible price. Your goal is to have less stuff after you sell, which means many things will sell for less than you hoped. For instance, I sold my $250 wedding dress online for the price of postage (10 years after we were married). Although I did not make money off the sale, someone has a wedding dress. We have reclaimed space in our home.

Be aware that some online selling services, such as Craig's List, have scammers. They will ask you to send them your items, and then they will mail you a check. The check may never arrive. They may mail you a check and ask you to ship the items, but the check bounces. Scammers use tricks like these to gain access to your belongings or your bank account. Pay attention to the warning signs and proceed with caution.

Distantly Related Family Researchers

For the documents, photos, and treasures that belong to the surnames you chose not to continue maintaining, you can seek out a family historian outside your immediate family members. Look for individuals actively researching a surname that is more closely related to the line, even though they are more distantly related to you.

Accomplish this by visiting the FamilySearch or Ancestry websites. On FamilySearch, look at the change history or source list for the names of users recently adding to an individual's profile. On Ancestry, search for member trees with the relevant surnames. Look for trees with the most sources and then review the user's profile to determine when they last logged into Ancestry.

Contact the potential relatives via the messaging system within FamilySearch and Ancestry. Describe the items you have and ask whether they would like to receive them. If they agree, mail the genealogical research or artifacts.

Genealogical Societies or Libraries

Consider donating your genealogy research to a relevant society or library. Search online for a genealogical society, historical society, library in the area where your relatives lived. Search for county or parish level, as well as the state level societies and libraries.

Review their website's donation policy or contact the organization directly. Some societies and libraries welcome city directories, county histories, yearbooks, and published family histories if they do not have a copy in their collection. Others only want original records about family lines from the area, while others will accept any genealogy research log, note, or record so long as it is organized. Some organizations are no longer accepting submissions. When in doubt, detail what you wish to donate and ask if the organizations would welcome the donation.

Most societies and libraries that welcome research donations request that you organize the documents that you submit. Organize your files to make your research readily available to other researchers.

For donations involving journals, diaries, and artifacts, include a pedigree chart and a few groups sheets to inform researchers who originally owned the object. If you know the story behind the item or have any transcripts, the organization receiving your donation may appreciate a paper copy of that as well.

You might be surprised about what items you can donate to libraries and museum collections. A history museum in Cedar Rapids, Iowa sought after historical pieces that help further their mission to "share the stories of our past, and connect people of all ages to the present and future of Linn County." The museum welcomes books, periodicals, and personal papers (such as letters, diaries, etc.) so long as those items relate to the culture of Linn County or the individuals who lived there.

They also accepted photographs, audiovisual materials, items manufactured in the county, and historical maps or architectural drawings of buildings from the area. They collect clothing items worn by individuals who lived in Cedar Rapids and the surrounding area. On a limited basis, they curated artifacts not specifically about Linn County. One curator told me that they collected toys from the 1920s so the library could show a typical childhood in the area, even if the toys did not belong to someone in Iowa.

Do not view history museums, university archives, and other repositories as the "Goodwill" for everything old. They will not accept any item they already have in their collection. If a donor sends material they have without previously contacting them, they will reject it. Archivists and curators will review and evaluate each item before agreeing to accept it. You will have to establish the antiquity of something to assist a museum or an archive in deciding whether the objects meet their requirements. The donation process could take weeks, months, or years. Avoid it if you do not have enough time.

I had a diary from the 1860s and a wallet full of historical snippets that belonged to a man who was on a distant family line. This man was the son of an original founder of a rural town in Ohio. I knew the man's family tree and their vital information, emphasizing the link to this rural town's founders. When visiting the Ohio State Archives, I asked if they would be interested in these items.

An archivist accepted the items for review and made a preliminary evaluation of the journal, wallet and the history I provided about the owner of the artifacts. Five years after making the donation, I received a notice formally accepting the items. An archivist had read the diary and found it insightful for Ohio history. This treasure lives on as part of the Ohio State Archive's history collection.

Local archives accept donations, as do state, regional, and national museums. History museums will often accept military uniforms from the Civil War, the Spanish American War, and World Wars. Since many soldiers brought back war trophies (firearms, uniforms, etc.) that have lain in family attics for decades, do not ignore museums about 'the other side.' Those museums may accept your donation to help them portray history more accurately. When our family visited Washington D.C., we visited the Antietam Battlefield. They had a lovely museum with artifacts belonging to the men, both Union and Confederate, that fought there. If you have something that belongs to soldiers that fought in specific battles and can prove they did, you could contact the museum located at that site about making a donation.

Some historic homes and villages accept donations that help them visually recreate a specific era even if the artifact is not the exact possessions that belonged to the historical figure featured.

What other places could you donate items of historical significance?

Investigate museums tailored to specific occupations, ethnicities, churches, manufactured items, and more. Universities also have special collections on a variety of topics. Search the internet for museums or universities in the areas your ancestors came from, where your items were manufactured, or organizations your ancestors were affiliated with.

My grandfather worked as a professor at Ohio State University. After contacting the Ohio State University special collections curator about potential personnel files for my grandfather, the curator expressed a desire for more heirs of former professors to consider contributing family documents and artifacts items to their holdings. If your relative has a connection to a university, ask about archivist interest in specific belongings you wish to donate.

Notice this process takes a considerable amount of time to donate a handful of items and papers. If you have a long timeline, utilize this avenue as a resource. If you have less than a month to downsize, skip this option.

Collectors

If you have items of historical significance or collectibles that are highly prized, you might find a private collector or use a broker. Only utilize this avenue for high-end items such as rare books, antiques, or artwork.

I inherited my mother's genealogical pile. The disorganized stack contained a few Mormon religious books published in the 1840s. My family lines do not have anyone who belonged to that religion, so the original owner of the books is unknown. Why my family had these books remains a mystery. Though poorly preserved, Andy set out to find a collector for the books.

Andy successfully found a collector who focused on 1820 - 1850 Americana artifacts, including Mormon books. He added our volumes to his collection. The collector described how he already had made arrangements with Yale University to take his collection when he dies.

Devon's mother had a difficult time finding collectors for her father's model train that consumed 75% of their garage. She advertised in model train magazines for buyers and only sold about half the collection. If Devon had to downsize her father's train collection, she would not have known that such magazines existed.

My brother had a comic book collection that he needed to downsize. Because of his familiarity with the collectibles, he could find buyers for his collection. If I had to downsize his collection, I would have gone to a comic book consignment store and taken whatever they offered.

Your ability to find collectors depend on your knowledge of the items, the potential collectors of such things, and the length of your timeline. You will not always find an interested collector when you need them. You might have to sell or give away your collectibles for less than you desire.

Not Every Treasure Can Be Given Away

The cold hard truth is many people have kept things that do not retain their value. For the most part, you filtered out these items and put them in the recycling bin during your initial downsizing. You should have filtered them further after you digitized your belongings. If you can not find someone to accept your belongings, you can always attempt to take them to the charitable donation center. However, it is possible you need to place them in the trash pile.

For instance, high school girls in Texas receive mums from their dates or family members to celebrate the football homecoming game. Outside of Texas, many people consider the homecoming mums ridiculous (Andy certainly does). I treasured my senior year artificial flower with streamers and noisy bells and whistles for 20 years after high school. It never came out of its box in the attic but had moved with us to three different states.

Finally, I took a photo of it and needed to give it a new home. Our kids could not play with it. No museum would take it. We could not donate it to charity or sell it online. I relented and placed my beloved homecoming mum in a trash bag and bid a fond farewell on trash day with a few tears in my eyes. Five years later, do I feel guilty? Not at all. We have the photos of the ridiculous fake flower (Andy's words, not mine) and I have included those in my high school scrapbooks to preserve my personal history.

Giving Takes Time

Your ability to find new homes for things depends on the length of your timeline to downsize. If you have 6 months or more, you can seek out collectors, museums, and archives. If you have a weekend, you will make multiple trips to a donation center.

Do not hold on to something just because you want to find the best collector for the item. Realistically examine your constraints and respond accordingly.

As you work through the items you give away, store them in disposable containers. Do not invest in archival quality boxes for the things you will not keep.

When you have emptied everything from the giveaway pile, the only pile that remains is the one marked Keep.

SHOWCASE: Display What You Love

Once you have reduced, preserved, and reclaimed the space in your home, and migrated from one place to another if applicable, you must now showcase your treasures. In so doing, you will enhance the value of your belongings such that others will also recognize their worth.

A line in one of my favorite movies spoke of a dress that had been boxed up for many years. The owner of the dress wanted a friend to wear it because "the dress has been in the box for so long, it deserves a night out."

That quote stuck with me as I decorated our home with our treasures. I showcase figurines from our trips to Taiwan and China, my two pageant crowns, trophies from Andy's karate wins, and more. Our home shows off my grandmother's religious icons and Andy's grandmother's movie star figurines. Throughout our bedroom, dining room, and the entrance to our home, we can see and appreciate our family history.

When you showcase your family history, you will focus on physical storage and sharing the legacy.

Physical Storage

Storage is a premium whether you live in an apartment in Manhattan, on a ranch in rural Texas, or a suburban two-story in San Diego. If you live outside of the United States, home storage becomes a further luxury. Therefore, when you surround yourself with the things you need and love, you should follow the Daily, Weekly, Monthly and Occasionally allocation system.

Store the belongings according to their functionality and how often you wish to view them.

Store items you use or wish to view daily in the easiest to reach storage places or in locations you spend the most time at eye level.

Store items used weekly within reach but out of the way of your frequently used items in the appropriate room for use. Display items you want to view less often in rooms in which you spend less time, but at eye level or in the rooms you spend the most time but place the items near the ceilings or low to the ground.

Store items used monthly in more difficult to access locations within the appropriate room for use or a hall closet. For the things you wish to see less frequently but do not want to pack away, place them in the rooms you use less often but in a location that is difficult to view.

Store items used or displayed occasionally in an out of the way storage location. When you need it, you will dig it out, no matter where you have placed it.

Organizing Your Household Items By Function

You use dinner plates and silverware daily. Place these items in the best drawers and the easiest to access shelves. You might also use an appliance such as a coffee maker or a blender. Keep these items on your countertop.

You may use specific dishes or appliances weekly, such as a casserole dish and a crock pot. Items such as these should not block access to anything you use daily. Place them on a higher shelf or in a lower cabinet.

Many kitchens have pots, pans and other items that are used once a month. We have a large stock pot that fits the bill. Store such items behind your more frequently used cookware, dinnerware, or other kitchen belongings. Keep them from hindering access to things you use daily or weekly.

Finally, think about special pans or serving dishes that you use annually or for a specific occasion. Where should these items go? For us, we have a cabinet that is difficult to access without a step stool or ladder. We store our Christmas candles and seasonal serving dishes there. If our kitchen had less cabinet space, we would store the seasonal items in a closet away from the kitchen.

Displaying Your Treasures By Sentimentality

Once your household items have a well-planned location, you should now showcase your family history. Place the essential things where you wish to view them often.

What pictures and keepsakes do you want to view every day? I want to see the calendar, our annual family picture, and an image of Jesus. The calendar hangs next to our refrigerator in our kitchen. The family portrait hangs above our television in the living room. The picture of Jesus hangs near the front entrance of our home so we can view it as we enter and leave. The photos appear at eye level or prominent spaces on our wall.

What do you want to notice weekly? We have a nook in our entryway where we can see souvenirs from our travels. We have a display in our dining room featuring awards we have received, my pageant crowns, and ceramic crafts the children have made. In our bedroom, we have photos of us in the early years of our marriage. We want to notice these things regularly, but they do not prevent us from viewing the pictures we want to see daily.

What do you want to view monthly? Most of us pass by pictures in hallways without noticing them, but we love the images on those walls. Use the halls for your treasures that you find value in but do not need to see as often as the other items you placed in the rooms at eye level. We have a hallway that has photos of extended family and some deceased ancestors.

If you have family history books, journals, or scrapbooks, keep them in view but not in the way of your everyday reading material. We placed a bookcase in our living room in a corner to house our family journals and scrapbooks. We put these books on the lowest and highest shelves. We remember they exist, but they do not block access to our library and school books. In short, you will want to have easy access to your treasures but do not hinder your access to things you use more frequently.

What do you want to access yearly? For us, our yearly decorations fall into the seasonal category. We bring the appropriate item out for holidays or special occasions. I have the christening gown and veil for my daughters in the back of our closet. I remember they exist and where they are located. When our daughters want to look at them, I can dig them out with ease. When our daughters need them for special days, I can find the veil and dress without too much difficulty.

How you decorate your home and store your treasures depends on where you live and the rooms you have available. Decorate according to how often you want or need to view your belongings to bring you joy.

Organizing Your Family History Research By Function

Your family history research should stay in one room as much as possible. For any genealogy project that you are touching daily, place the material within easy reach. Consider having a file on a desk, the first file in a drawer, or an easy to reach bin on a shelf.

For items that you will access once a week, you should place them slightly out of reach of your workspace. These items will likely be reference materials, research guides, and methodology books. Place these items on a shelf next to your workspace. Place notes behind your active research project in a file drawer. Do not block your access to your current project with things you only need once a week.

For binders, files, and archive boxes that you wish to access throughout the month as the need arises, place them slightly out of reach. Place your surname files behind your active project and your reference materials. Place your archival boxes on more difficult to reach shelves. You should not have to move long-term storage items to access a current project or frequently used reference material

For items you are preserving according to archival standards, place them in hard to reach places, such as closets or the highest shelves. Purposely use areas that require a ladder or stool to access. If you need something, you will step on the ladder to reach it.

Should you display that?

Do not hesitate to put photos, bibles, old clothing, and other keepsakes on display even though an archivist may shout at you, or me for the suggestion. If you always have these items in storage, they will lose their value as your family forgets their existence.

When your family sees the family treasures often, they gain familiarity with them. This increases their value. One friend has the Stetson hat that belonged to her ranch hand father. Throughout her childhood, she saw that hat hooked on the post of the dining room chair when her daddy came home. When he left, he took the hat with him. After his passing, she hung the cowboy hat on a chair post in her living room. Many suggested that she place the hat in a storage box so that others will have it long after her passing. She ignored this advice and kept the Stetson hat in view for all of her relatives. When she passed away, family members fought over who would inherit their grandpa's hat. They wanted to feel connected to their grandfather and their mother thanks to the cowboy hat always remaining in view.

Sharing the Legacy

After you decorate and organize your home, you should consider how you can share your family legacy for your family to enjoy now and long into the future.

Create Wall Displays

Have wall space, will decorate with family history. A variety of family history displays showcase your possessions. You could make or purchase a metal family tree and use magnets to mount your family photos. You could line a wall with several parallel partial shelves. Place photos and artifacts on the shelves to celebrate your heritage.

I made a shadow box family tree. Inside I has a portrait of a couple, the names and marriage date of each, and then artifacts that belonged one of the members. The 'tree' begins with us at the bottom with Andy's Eagle Scout award and my color guard medallions. The row above us has shadow boxes for our parents, and then our grandparents appear above. Each box has jewelry, charms, or patches that represent someone in the couple.

Use your creativity to arrange frames, shadow boxes and other items into wall and shelf displays. Show off your photos, documents, and keepsakes that feature your family history.

Viewing the Files on Your TV

Turn your TV into a digital picture frame. With your photos, slides, and video clips digitized, you can now view them anytime you wish through your TV. You can insert a thumb drive of your favorite photos and select the folder to view or access a folder from a cloud drive. With minimal effort you have a place to view these images any time you have the TV on slideshow mode.

Share the Files

Pass on your family legacy by sharing the digital files you created with your family members. Give them copies of the digitized photos, documents, genealogical databases, audio files, and video clips. The technology of sharing such data is ever changing so you will want to research the latest formats used. As of this printing, sharing files on thumb drives, external hard drives or through cloud storage are the norm. DVDs and CDs are quickly becoming obsolete as many computers no longer have these drives installed.

Print the Journal

In the digitization section, we recommend that you scan or photograph diaries or journals and then transcribe the content. Take that project one step further and format the transcription into a book.

Format the text for a 6x9 inch book for easy shelving and reading. Create a cover page and a page providing background details about the author of the journal and perhaps some pictures of the people or places discussed within. Export the book to a PDF file and then upload the file to an on-demand book printing service. As of this printing, Lulu.com and Amazon are two of our favorite resources to publish such books at a reasonable price. You can order one copy or 100 with no minimum purchase required. A 90-page softcover 6x9 in book costs less than $5 to print, plus the cost of shipping.

Write a Book

It may sound daunting, but writing a book about your ancestors or yourself can pass on the legacy of those who have gone before.

Our children love when we read aloud the story of how Grandpa Bert flew from Kelly Air Force Base to China "the long way around." Thankfully we have that story recorded in a Lee Family History Book.

I wrote a biography about my Grandpa Lew Brown. My aunt enjoyed the book so much that she purchased copies for children, grandchildren, and great-grandchildren!

Books are treasures so long as they have stories and photos inside. If you need help writing those stories, we have written a book that simplifies and speeds up the process. It is called, *A Recipe for Writing Family History*.

After you write the book, upload it Lulu.com, or other on-demand services, and order the copies you need. They make great holiday gifts.

Create Photo Books and Scrapbooks

If you think writing a book is too challenging, start writing about your family by creating photo books or scrapbooks.

Photo books differ from scrapbooks in that they arrange pictures much the same way we do in traditional photo albums. Photo books have less decorative elements than scrapbooks. Avoid printing photo books that lack captions or stories. You can digitally recreate a photo album and add details about each picture below or beside the images.

One photo book could feature the collection you reduced. Showcase a photo or several photos of an item from the collection on one page and on the facing page describe the item or the story behind how you received it. You could choose a color scheme for the background pages for the overall book or stick to black or white.

For scrapbooks, you will pair short stories with photos of your ancestors. Short stories may be a paragraph or two in length. Then you surround that short memory or story with pictures. For multiple paragraph stories, place the text on one page and photos on the facing page.

Scrapbooks do not have to be overly complicated or decorative. When you focus on the photos and the stories, a few colored papers and decorative elements highlight the subject of the story.

Topics of photobook and scrapbook projects:

- Feature one ancestor and the photos from their life.
- Feature the letters exchanged between a couple.
- Feature recipes and the stories about with them.
- Feature the collection you photographed during the preservation chapter and then reduced. Share the stories behind each collected piece
- Feature a home and the memories that happened there.

The trick to photo books and scrapbooks is to keep the focus of the project narrow. One person, one couple, one event (even if over several decades), or one collection should be the subject of each separate book. Creating a large family history consumes too many pages and makes these projects not only overwhelming to create but also to flip through. Keep these projects simple so you can be successful. If you have too much content for a photo book, then you are ready to create a paperback or hardback book (without the decorations).

Create Audio or Visual Documentaries

If you have audio or video files, use them to their fullest advantage and create documentaries about the subject of those recordings. Keep the videos short, meaning less than 15 minutes.

Reserve longer documentaries for celebrities or significant historical events. When it comes to your ancestors, you want to tell short stories for two reasons. The first is they are easy to consume by the family members who may or may not be interested in their legacy. You can create multiple stories about an ancestor, family, or place and string these together to tell a longer story. If you have the life history of a British Immigrant who has died, one story could be about the migration to his new home. Another story could be about how he met his wife. Perhaps another story could be about his occupation.

The second reason to create short videos is that they require fewer computer resources. When I created the 3-minute video story called *A Journey to Belonging* about how family history helps me feel connected, our computer often crashed because of the number of graphic resources required to make the short clip. Longer and more complex videos need more computer resources than most people have available.

When you create your videos, allow the interviews, music performance recordings, and video clips dictate the videos or audio documentaries that you create. Add a little background music and historical context to make the experience more enjoyable. Utilize the photos of the pictures, documents, and keepsakes to enhance the viewing experience.

There are a variety of video editing programs available. Find the one that is the easiest for you to understand and utilize to create your stories. If your tech skills are limited, invite a family member to help you or hire someone to create your projects.

Showcase

You can spend the remainer of your life after downsizing in the showcasing phase. You should have moved to your new location or finished processing your inherited files.

Every way you showcase your family history from this point forward adds to the value of the family history items you have preserved because your family will see that you value those artifacts.

Peace from Downsizing

When you have less - you have more!

When you downsize through the filter of functionality and long-term family history value, you ultimately have fewer possessions, but those items have the greatest genealogical, sentimental and serviceable value.

When we clean out our children's rooms, we often walk them through this process with their own things. We keep what they still use and enjoy. We preserve the items with the greatest sentimental or personal history value. We give new homes to everything else. When we are finished, their rooms have significantly fewer physical objects, yet they enjoy the things that remain with less frustration. You can downsize much the same way.

An additional benefit of downsizing with family history in mind is the peace of being prepared when disaster threatens or strikes.

We lived through Hurricane Harvey's destruction on Houston and surrounding areas in 2017. When the flood of 2008 hit Cedar Rapids, Iowa, we lived there as well. Our hearts broke as neighbors, coworkers, associates, and total strangers stacked their waterlogged, mold-infested or charred belongings on the curb. The trash mountains along the curbs in their neighborhoods tormented them for many weeks before the removal trucks hauled it all away. Tears continuously streamed as they looked at the furniture, bedding, and papers that they could no longer enjoy.

A workshop attendee shared one of the most heart wrenching stories we have heard. A week before Hurricane Harvey hit Houston, she had decided to pull out and digitize a family photo album created in the 1860s. The photo album contained pictures of her ancestors who served as soldiers during the Civil War. The flood waters damaged the only copy of these photos in existence. She lamented that she had not thought to take the album with her when she fled her home for safety or had digitized the photos years earlier.

Other friends have wept as they removed their high school treasures from their flooded basements. They did not necessarily need the keepsakes, but they wish they had done a better job of preserving their memories.

My grandparent's estate generated a family feud that involved a court trial. In the end, few artifacts remained from their hunting hobby, family photos and documents, heirlooms, and the artwork my grandfather created. Years later I discovered a few photo albums in the care of a second cousin. Shortly after the discovery, the cousin's home burned down, and the family treasures were lost again.

Reducing, organizing and preserving your possessions enables you to leave your home quickly when disaster strikes but save your family history. If you have a fire, you grab your organized box of original documents and photos and flee. If your evacuation timeline expands from minutes to hours, you can grab previously mentioned box along with additional irreplaceable family history gold items. Your only limit is the space your vehicle permits.

If you cannot save your family photo albums, you can rest easy knowing you have a backup. If your photos reside on your laptop, you will grab that as you flee your home. Your digitized photos will remain on your computer, on a thumb drive or external hard drive, or in cloud storage until you are ready to create reprints when you settle into a new location.

Another side benefit of downsizing and preserving your possessions in digital form, you also have the evidence of your belongings for your insurance claims. Those pictures can help you replace items in your home. Imagine the peace you will fill with this added protection against disasters.

Downsize As If You Were Dying Next Month

A popular cliche suggests you "live like you are dying." We advise you to downsize as if you had one month left to live. No one knows or values your stuff more than you do. But with the right plan, you can share that value and those memories with others.

Downsize with a view towards preserving your treasures, legacy, and life's work for your posterity. Even after you filter the chrome plastic from the gold, there are no guarantees you will succeed. However, you improve the odds your family history lives on when you reduce, preserve, reclaim, and showcase.

Action Plans

The following Action Plans are designed help you in your downsizing. They can be ripped out of the book, pasted on a wall or workspace and implemented.

Additionally, we referenced several Quick Guides throughout the book. These don't fit the size format of this book very well so use this web address to access the PDF file for them:

http://bit.ly/DownsizingCheatSheets

The Quick Guides are designed to be printed, (enough for all those helping you downsize), and consulted while each person works independently. This file will be periodically updated and expanded. The link above contains the following quick reference guides:

- Downsizing: 1-Hour Action Plan (included in this book)
- Downsizing: Weekend Action Plan (included in this book)
- Downsizing: 3-5 Month Action Plan (included in this book)
- Downsizing: 12 Month Action Plan (included in this book)
- \<Blank> Surname Table
- Quick Guide to Sorting Possessions
- Quick Guide to Processing Papers and Photos
- Basic Assessment
- Expanded Assessment – Master Bedroom
- Expanded Assessment – Bedroom
- Expanded Assessment – Bathroom
- Expanded Assessment – Office
- Expanded Assessment – Kitchen
- Expanded Assessment – Dining Room
- Expanded Assessment – \<Blank>

DOWNSIZING: 1-HOUR ACTION PLAN

Start with Step 1 and work your way through the list. Sign off each item once it is complete so that you know where you are at in the process. If working with others, after a room has been photographed, extra helpers can begin Steps 2-6 for that room while you continue with Step 1.

1. _____ Photograph home before downsizing begins.

   a) _____ Photograph each room and the large details.

   b) _____ Photograph prized collections as a whole.

2. _____ Keep photos (loose, organized, framed, albums, or envelopes).

3. _____ Keep genealogy binders, file folders, and family history books (if possible).

4. _____ Keep documents, media, and family history books.

5. _____ Keep jewelry.

6. _____ Keep a few sentimental items or collections with 3-5 items.

7. _____ Give away any previously determined or specified inheritance items to heirs.

As time permits, you can keep lifestyle items, clothing and small furnishings.

When the time ends, you leave the rest to work crews to donate to charity or sell as they see fit.

DOWNSIZING: WEEKEND ACTION PLAN

Start with Step 1 and work your way through the list. Sign off each item once it is complete so that you know where you are at in the process. If working with others, after a room has been photographed, extra helpers can begin Steps 2-10 for that room while you continue with Step 1. Steps that are labeled as "Give Away" are to family heirs or charitable donation centers. You won't have time to donate to other places.

1. _____ Photograph home before downsizing begins.

    a) _____ Photograph each room and the large details.

    b) _____ Photograph prized collections as a whole.

2. _____ Move furnishings, clothing, and lifestyle items essential for living to new space.

3. _____ Give away any previously determined or specified inheritance items to heirs.

4. _____ Rapidly sort through remaining furnishings and clothing. Keep only items that of genealogy gold.

5. _____ Give away remaining furnishings and clothing in good condition to charity collection centers.

6. _____ Trash furnishings and clothing that are broken or are unacceptable to charity collection centers (such as TVs or undergarments).

7. Collections:

    a) _____ Reduce prized collections to 5-10 favorite pieces.

    b) _____ Give away or Trash the rest.

8. Photos:

   a) _____ Rapidly sort through photos loose, envelopes, framed, or albums for identified individuals.

   b) _____ Keep only pictures that can be identified, no matter the surname.

   c) _____ Trash all photos and photo albums with unidentified individuals that you do not recognize personally.

9. Documents:

   a) _____ Rapidly sort through document piles, files, and binders.

   b) _____ Keep only the original documents and images.

   c) _____ Keep only charts that have sources on them.

   d) _____ Trash all genealogy papers that contain notes, photocopies, and family group sheets with no identified sources.

10. Media:

    a) _____ Keep story-based family history books, home movies, slides, and negatives.

    b) _____ Trash books, magazines, and movies according to cheat sheet.

    c) _____ Trash remaining clutter

DOWNSIZING: 3-5 MONTH ACTION PLAN

Start with Step 1 and work your way through the list. Sign off each item once it is complete so that you know where you are at in the process. If working with others, after a room has been photographed, extra helpers can begin Steps 2-5 for that room while you continue with Step 1. You may have time to find family members interested in your genealogy files or genealogical societies and archives. Your search for such recipients will be shallow.

Three - Five Months Before Downsize Deadline

1. _____ Photograph home before downsizing begins.
   a) _____ Photograph each room and the large details.
   b) _____ Photograph key dinnerware pieces.
   c) _____ Photograph treasured clothing items individually.
   d) _____ Photograph sentimental home decor items individually

2. Collections:
   a) _____ Photograph prized collections as a whole.
   b) _____ Photograph collection items individually.
   c) _____ Reduce prized collections to 5-10 favorite pieces.
   d) _____ Give away collections that will be gold to someone else:
      • Family Members
      • Garage / Estate Sales
      • Online selling sites
      • Charity collection centers
   e) _____ Trash the rest

3. Documents:
   a) _____ Give away binders and files for family lines you not longer wish to maintain to genealogy libraries or historical societies.

DOWNSIZING: 3-5 MONTH ACTION PLAN (continued)

b) ____ Give away binders and files to family members interested in the work.

c) ____ Process the piles, files, binders, for any family line you are actively researching.

d) ____ Trash all papers that photocopies, and family group sheets with no identified sources.

e) ____ Keep original or near-original genealogical document.

f) ____ When in doubt about the value of a paper, keep it to process later.

g) ____ Process family group sheets that have sources. Once information is in a digital tree, trash these sheets.

h) ____ Place images in the photo piles.

i) ____ Reduce the organization of the papers to the fewest files or binders as possible.

j) ____ Trash all papers that are photocopies, and family group sheets on abandoned family lines.

k) ____ Trash all other papers based on the Quick Guide to Processing Papers and Photos.

4. Photos:

a) ____ Trash blurry, duplicate, or inappropriate photos.

b) ____ Trash photos with an unclear or confusing purpose.

c) ____ Keep photos that are labeled.

d) ____ Process photos that are not labeled.

e) ____ Give away unidentified photos to websites like DeadFred.com.

f) ____ Trash all photos and photo albums with unidentified individuals that you were unable to determine in 3-5 months.

5. Media:

   a) _____ Process slides and negatives by reducing collection to slides and negatives that depict people and buildings.

   b) _____ Trash slides and negatives that do not meet the above standard.

   c) _____ Temporarily reduce their storage containers for slides and negatives until digitization is complete.

   d) _____ Process book, magazine, and movie collection by photographic the collections as a whole.

   e) _____ Photograph a few unique or notable items.

   f) _____ Trash books, magazines, and movies.

   g) _____ Keep story-based family history books and home movies.

   h) _____ Trash chart based family histories.

   i) _____ Keep genealogy methodology and resource books that you are actively using.

   j) _____ Trash outdated genealogy methodology and resource books.

One - Two Months Before Downsize Deadline

6. Furnishing, Housewares, Clothing, Personal Effects:

   a) _____ Give away any previously determined or specified inheritance items to heirs.

   b) _____ Keep furnishings, clothing, and lifestyle items essential items you will move to use in the new space.

   c) _____ Keep furnishings, clothing, and lifestyle items that fit in the new space and have sentimental value.

d) _____ Give away furnishings, clothing, personal effects that will be gold to someone else:

- Family Members
- Garage / Estate Sales
- Charity collection centers

e) _____ Trash large furnishings, clothing, personal effects, and home decor from the home that are broken, do not sell, or are unacceptable to charity collection centers.

Week of Downsize Deadline

7. _____ Move furnishings, clothing, and lifestyle items to new space.

8. _____ Trash remaining clutter.

DOWNSIZING: 12 MONTH ACTION PLAN

Start with Step 1 and work your way through the list. Sign off each item once it is complete so that you know where you are at in the process. If working with others, after a room has been photographed, extra helpers can begin Steps 2-5 for that room while you continue with Step 1. You may have time to find family members interested in your genealogy files or genealogical societies and archives. Your search for such recipients will be shallow.

Six to Twelve Months Before Downsize Deadline

1. _____ Photograph home before downsizing begins.
   a) _____ Photograph each room and the finer details.
   b) _____ Photograph large furnishings individually.
   c) _____ Photograph key dinnerware pieces.
   d) _____ Photograph treasured clothing items individually.
   e) _____ Photograph sentimental home decor items individually.

2. Collections:
   a) _____ Photograph prized collections as a whole.
   b) _____ Photograph collection items individually.
   c) _____ Photograph individual keepsakes.
   d) _____ Reduce prized collections to 5-10 favorite pieces.
   e) _____ Give away collections that will be gold to someone else:
   - Family Members
   - Garage / Estate Sales
   - Find collectors or museums
   - Charity collection centers.
   f) _____ Trash the rest.

DOWNSIZING: 12 MONTH ACTION PLAN (continued)

3. Documents:

   a) _____ Give away binders and files you no longer wish to maintain to family members interested in the work.

   b) _____ Give away binders and files you no longer wish to maintain to researchers actively working on the line that you discover through connections on genealogy websites.

   c) _____ Give away binders and files for family lines you no longer wish to maintain to genealogy libraries or historical societies.

   d) _____ Process the piles, files, and binders, for any family line you are actively researching.

   e) _____ Trash all papers that are photocopies and family group sheets with no identified sources.

   f) _____ Remove images from folders and place images in the photo piles.

   g) _____ Process family group sheets that have sources on them by adding information to digitized tree. Trash the charts when finished.

   h) _____ Process copies of documents by comparing them to online sources. If they are online, discard the papers. If they are not, keep digitize the documents then trash the photo copies.

   i) _____ Keep original or near-original genealogical documents.

   j) _____ Reduce the organization of the papers to the fewest files or binders as possible.

   k) _____ Trash all other papers based on Downsizing Quick Guides.

4. Photos:

   a) _____ Trash blurry, duplicate, or inappropriate photos.

   b) _____ Trash photos with an unclear or confusing purpose.

   c) _____ Keep photos that are labeled.

   d) _____ Process photos that are not labeled by asking family members what they know, organizing photos to see if you can determine who the individual was, or posting in online forums.

   e) _____ Give away unidentified photos to archives, libraries, or genealogical societies (if applicable).

   f) _____ Post images on websites like Dead Fred to find possible leads.

   g) _____ Trash all photos and photo albums with unidentified individuals that you were unable to determine in 12 months.

5. Media:

   a) _____ Process slides and negatives by sifting through the images and keeping only the ones that depict people and buildings.

   b) _____ Trash the remaining slides and negatives.

   c) _____ Digitize slides and negatives by outsourcing the project.

   d) _____ Trash the slides and negative after they are digitized. (You could keep them in archival boxes of reduced size only if you have space to maintain the photos in your new space.)

   e) _____ Photograph book, magazine, movie, and music collections as a whole.

   f) _____ Photograph individual historically significant items.

g) _____ Keep genealogy methodology and resource books that you are actively using.

h) _____ Keep story-based family history books and home movies.

i) _____ Find a collector or museum for historical media.

j) _____ Trash books, magazines, movies, music.

k) _____ Trash chart based family histories.

l) _____ Trash outdated genealogy methodology and resource books.

m) _____ Digitize home movies, audio recording, performances of relatives.

n) _____ Trash the decaying media after digitization is complete.

One to Six Months Before Downsize Deadline

6. Furnishing, Housewares, Clothing, Lifestyle Items:

a) _____ Give away any previously determined or specified inheritance items to heirs.

b) _____ Keep furnishings, clothing, and lifestyle items essential items you will move to use in the new space.

c) _____ Keep furnishings, clothing, and lifestyle items that fit in the new space and have sentimental value.

d) _____ Give away furnishings, clothing, personal effects that will be gold to someone else: Family Members, Museums or Collectors, Garage / Estate Sales, Online selling sites, Charity collection centers.

e) _____ Trash large furnishings, clothing, personal effects, and home decor from the home that are broken, do not sell, or are unacceptable to charity collection centers.

7. Finish processing Documents, Photos, and Media.

DOWNSIZING: 12 MONTH ACTION PLAN (continued)

Week of Downsize Deadline

8. _____ Move furnishings, clothing, and lifestyle items to new space.

9. _____ Trash remaining clutter.

About the Authors

Devon Noel Lee specializes in preserving and sharing family memories and motivating budding genealogists. She has created and published 60 scrapbooks, written a memoir from her teenage years and four family history how-to books, including the popular *A Recipe for Writing Family History*. She has written the stories for over 120 ancestors and counting and is working on compiling many of them into a book. Devon is a high energy speaker and lab instructor at local, state, national genealogy conferences and public libraries. She educates and inspires the genealogy world through videos at FamilyHistoryFanatics.com. She graduated from Texas A&M with degrees in Marketing and Journalism. Currently, Devon is a home educator for five superheroes.

Andy Lee has been involved in family history for 30 years and wrote a contest winning essay about an American Revolution ancestor while in high school. As a member of Toastmaster's International, Andy has achieved the status of Competent Communicator and won several storytelling contests. He has given presentations throughout the US and Canada to professional organizations, university classes, local genealogy societies, family history conferences, and Boy Scout organizations. He's the co-author of *A Recipe for Writing Family History* and contributes to the FamilyHistoryFanatics.com YouTube channel. Andy graduated from Texas A&M University with a degree in Mechanical Engineering.

Made in the USA
Middletown, DE
22 November 2019